200 YEARS OF GRINGOS

Carlos Alberto Montaner

Translated by
Gastón Fernández de la Torriente
James F. Horton

UNIVERSITY PRESS OF AMERICA

LANHAM • NEW YORK • LONDON

University Press of America,™ Inc.

4720 Boston Way
Lanham, MD 20706

3 Henrietta Street
London WC2E 8LU England

Printed in the United States of America

Library of Congress Cataloging in Publication Data

Montaner, Carlos Alberto.
200 years of gringos.

Translation of: 200 años de gringos.
1. United States–Civilization–1945– . 2. United States–Territorial expansion. 3. United States–Foreign relations–20th century. I. Title. II. Title: Two hundred years of gringos.
E169.12.M6413 1983 973.9 83–12373
ISBN 0–8191–3374–4 (alk. paper)
ISBN 0–8191–3375–2 (pbk. : alk. paper)

to my wife Linda

Table of Contents

PROLOGUE

This book was perpetrated under the pretext of the bicentennial of the United States as an independent nation. As I wrote it, it was published in bits and pieces in numerous newspapers in Spain, North and South America including the United States and Brazil, and was potentially read by two to three million people. Consequently it has none of the mystery of virginity that accompanies those texts that are scrupulously kept secret until they are published, but it does have the appeal of a striptease in that things are revealed little by little. Viewed from the perspective of a book, these essays take on coherence and unity. From experience, I can predict the reaction of many readers: shock. I'm sorry. Many others will eventually agree with its essential arguments. That's the fate of any essay which attempts to avoid the commonplace.

The book deals with several polemic essays revolving around the *Gringos* and also around us, us Spanish-speaking fauna. In my opinion the tremendous importance of the Americans doesn't lie in the fact that they have become the most powerful country on earth, but that no matter where we go we run into them. In that case the wisest thing to do is to talk about them in relationship to us and about us in relationship to them. I'm not sure this can be termed a method, but it's the only one used in this book. I simply point out a few aspects of these people that are of interest to us, and I discuss them candidly.

But there's more; there are some propositions of a universal nature concerning violence, time, competition, technology, and aggression which transcend mere exegesis. This book attempts to go beyond describing what *Gringos* are like on their two hundredth birthday. It's a series of essays of a sociological, political, anthropological or historical nature--or a little of each--desperately clinging to the classic definition of the genre: hypothesis without demonstration. I don't prove anything. I don't demonstrate anything. I simply observe and tell what I think I see. I figure that this won't amount to very much in our age of perforated computer cards, but I don't know how nor am I interested in "essaying" in a more scientific fashion, and I harbor depressing suspicions about any attempt to fix, ensnare, or define any nation between the covers of a book.

Someone says "the Germans" and you don't know whether he's talking about Goethe or Adolf Hitler or Martin Borman or Albert Einstein. You hear "the Spaniards" and some people are referring to Saint Teresa and others are talking about La Pasionaria. I mention "the Gringos" and the reader rightly feels perplexed. He may wonder whether I'm talking about George Wallace or Martin Luther King or Al Capone or Cardinal Spellman. Nevertheless, as the saying goes, we are condemned to understand each other. In spite of everything there is a universal language of prejudices and conceptualizations that more or less all of us come to master. The reader, aware he hasn't bought a cookbook and knowing more or less what this book is about, will have to be somewhat of an accomplice in this reading. He will have to overlook the lack of statistics, mathematical tables and other signs of erudition. I don't feel like fooling with all that crap. "You lie more than statistics," says Mafalda,[1] the bitter Argentine philosopher. By "essaying" in this fashion, void of figures, I run the risk--which I haven't forgotten--of making a mistake, but not of lying.

Now let's talk about the Yankees. And about us.

* * *

The image of the United States that prevails in Spain and Latin America corresponds with the one held by Rodó's[2] Caliban. A spiritually barbarous nation that sees everything as a tool for acquisition of material goods. Once the Ariel-Caliban dichotomy that Rodo proposed was perversely distorted, the Yankees in the caricature were reduced to uncouth Coca-Cola addicts, a bunch of stupid people chewing on wads of gum, or a bunch of ignoramuses whose nerve centers were totally non-functional except in those areas that control commerce.

Paradoxically this grotesque image resulted from the most serious philosophical thought hatched in the United States: pragmatism. Pragmatism was the legitimate offspring of utilitarianism and positivism. More than philosophical speculation about existence, it turned out to be a system of values that established a hierarchy and a scale of priorities among things. Goods were valued according to the good they produced while "good" was defined in terms of pleasure and pleasure was identified only within the realm of comfort.

This perspective of man and life was squeezed into the monster Caliban so that it could be assimilated by the masses. But it turned out that Caliban, the pragmatic monster, began to take up strange habits. He founded symphonic orchestras, ballet companies, literary magazines, theatrical groups. In the halls of his universities (some three thousand) they studied not only disciplines allied with his philosophy but all human activities worthy of consideration. What irritated Ariel was knowing that Harvard had more books on Guatemala than the University of San Carlos. Or that last year Princeton and the University of Nebraska graduated more experts on Latin American Literature than the University of Havana.

Caliban cultivated the myth of the comfort society where the possession of objects granted status to a citizen at the same time that those very citizens, contradictorily, were acquiring an awareness of spiritual values. Caliban was beginning to be a little like Ariel. This book deals with those transformations.

* * *

"No one bathes twice in the same river," declared Heraclitus of Ephesus. The observation of the philosopher--at one time--was simple and eloquent. Reality is unstable; forever in perpetual transformation, changing, protean. Things, more than merely being, are in the process of being. The Greek's dictum fits the United States to a T; no one lives two consecutive days in the same Yankee country. There, instead of traveling through the world, one has the sensation that the world is traveling through him.

The profound revolution that is taking place on American soil has no parallel on the face of the earth. The appearances of cities are being leveled in a matter of hours, and cities are built in days; even the chemical composition of the air is different from the rest of the planet because millions of cars and factories see to it that the air is rarified. In addition, there is cultural pollution. Experimental laboratories daily turn out thousands of conclusions that transform the basic concepts of sciences and, at a tremendous speed, alter the rhythm of learning.

In the United States scholars go to bed every night with the fear of waking up totally ignorant.

Those of us who are ignorant sleep sound as logs and are happy to be surprised by whatever changes may come along. American law--simple ,a little bit clumsy if you like--has the necessary flexibility to adapt to change. The Constitution is moving along with difficulty, but at least it moves. (Perhaps the defect of our Law--which is Rome plus Spain plus Napoleon-- lies in its formal perfection, its minute explanation.)

Up until this point, the Yankee revolution was merely external. But there are inner changes much more transcendent. For years now the "capitalism" of classic rhetoric has hardly been heard of. The relationship between worker, production, and amount of work produced is submitted to an indefatigable dialectic that is constantly changing the framework of the economy. The ethical precepts--part of the tenets of Anglo-Saxon protestantism--become more and more hazy. The morality without dogmas that the justly forgotten Ingenieros[3] extolled is making a brilliant comeback. It still seems unlikely that they will go to the extreme proposed by Marcuse (a society without dogmas and without inhibitions of any kind), but the stampede is headed in that direction.

There is an enormous difference between the mentality of an American youth and that of his father; as great as the distance found between a Christian concept and a pagan one. Christianity has left the new pagans with a fraternal outlook toward their fellow men. In spite of everything, the heart-rending cry of Christianity--"love thy neighbor as thyself"--continues to reverberate in the conscience of Humanity--although at times it sounds like an energetic reproach.

The country constantly changes its repertoire of manners and attitudes. Basically the secret is simple; dogmas have been abolished. It's the first time this phenomenon has happened within a nation. Up until now only a few individuals had been able to shake loose the bridles of dogmatic thought. In the United States it's now happening as a collective experience among the young generation.

All this should put Spain and Latin America on guard. It would be ridiculous to continue judging the Yankees with Rodonesque rhetoric or with Marxist jargon. To talk seriously about this country--and not resort to classic commonplaces--we have to put our ears to the ground and listen carefully. We have to rise above our age old grudges, shade our eyes with our hands and observe with fairness. To go on wrapped up in our old prejudices is totally absurd. Our judgments--in order not to be irrational--should flow like Heraclitus' river or like the world of the Yankees.

NOTES

[1] Mafalda. Cartoon character.

[2] Jóse Enrique Rodó (1871-1917). Uruguayan writer and humanist. In his most important work, Ariel, Calibán represents materialism.

[3] José Ingenieros (1877-1925). Argentine sociologist and psychiatrist credited with introducing positivism into Argentina.

I

AMERICANIZATION OF THE PLANET

THE BIG BANG THAT NEVER STOPPED

July 1976 marked the 200th anniversary of the American Declaration of Independence. The contractions, rhythm and general nature of that birth in Philadelphia left an indelible mark on the infant. Let me explain what I mean by this. To have cast aside monarchy and to have subscribed to the superstition of democratic arithmetic was an astonishing event without precedent. Washington, Jefferson, and the rest of the crew innovated. _Innovate_, of course, is based on the Latin word for _new_. A _new_ system was initiated. In other words, they invented the time period in which they were living. They didn't look back to the past. They didn't copy. They didn't modify. They created. And by creating at the exact moment of birth, they implanted in the genetic makeup of their citizenry an irrepressible urgency for change and orginality.

For two hundred years that country has done precisely that: create. The initial surge has not diminished. The first big bang still has that universe expanding on the same course. The _Gringos_ don't look back; they create. They create incessantly. There is no characteristic more important in the makeup of that nation. The rest of the planet depends on that awesome peculiarity. They are the ones out front; the ones who determine the speed at which we travel, the diseases we cure, and even our topics of conversation.

For many years now almost everything that has been thought of in the world has been thought of in English. And I say this sadly. Humiliated. Annoyed. Spanish is a language used for cheap songs and dime novels. A system of communication which is used either for translating or humming. And the latter only occasionally, because lately our natives have taken to singing rock--or whatever it's called--in English.

When you hear "leader of nations" referring to the United States, you immediately think of its planes and its bombs. How absurd! Leadership isn't derived from a big club worn on your hip. The United States became a leader because of the research done in her laboratories, her unbelievable creativity, and her uncanny ability to change. For two centuries, by God, those fellows have been inventing the world! What idiot would even entertain the idea that it's possible to catch up with them? When we get to point X with our tongues hanging out, they'll no longer be there. They will already have left with their protean society which, Indian-like, is always ready to move on in pursuit of more comfortable and complex destinies.

There's not even a chance to desert or to return, like Gandhi, to the distaff and family plot abandoning all the electric gadgets. The bonds of modern communication are too strong. It's practically an act of cultural promiscuity for a person in Nicaragua to watch the obscene image of the moon landing on his home set. His mere possession of a TV set borders on being a cruel joke. But in any case it's inevitable. There's no way to stop up the cracks. The magic flute of Gringo leadership filters into our every pore. We are condemned to be followers.

Can we talk seriously about the decline of the United States? Yes, if we are talking about the petty political world. But seen from a perspective formed over the centuries, the Yankees have been important for humanity not because they won two world wars or because they lost in Angola, Vietnam or Cuba, but because they have elevated their values to a universal level and because they have impregnated everybody with their American way of life. And because they have caused everyone to copy their inventions, translate their texts and imitate their manners. In their role of father-creator, which is truly the most vital one, there is not one iota of decline. Quite to the contrary, as they abandon their role of world policeman, the country's internal vitality should increase. When the Linus Paulings and the Noam Chomskys become bored, they will do research. In other words, their time will be devoted to changing the world. (Ironically, their efforts will further widen the gap between the developed and underdeveloped countries.)

July 1976 was her 200th anniversary. I, for one, don't intend to be included among those who suffer from that absurd anti-Yankee phobia. I prefer being accused of selling myself to Wall Street by journalistic and literary chatterboxes than being taken for a fool. Realizing that I belong to a subsidiary world, one pulled along by another, already causes me sufficient bitterness without having salt rubbed in the wound by short-sighted schemes of latrine revolutionaries. I admire creativity whatever its source. And I deeply regret that our insignificant little world--one that speaks Spanish and prays to Jesus Christ, as poor old Rúben Darió[1] said--doesn't take up the scepter of leadership. I truly regret it.

THE GREAT STANDARDIZER

The USA is a neurotic Midas. Everything it touches becomes uniform. If we were talking about a satellite nation, it wouldn't matter. But since we are dealing with a nation that is a world leader, the implications are serious.

Let's start with the country itself. The most surprising aspect of that nation with its diversity of race, geography, and inhabitants is its uniformity. It's the same country whether you're in the deserts of Nevada, the pastures of Montana, or the Appalachian Mountains. The same gas stations, the same supermarkets, the same eating habits, the same churches, the same press. The same people.

Need I emphasize the fact that we are talking about a nation with 9,000,000 sq. kilometers, different climates, peaks and valleys which shelter 225 million souls coming from all possible racial and cultural mixtures? There the cultural mosaic becomes a monolith. A monochrome. Monotonous. Everything flat and alike.

Now that is boring, but it's also beneficial. Nowadays the borders between states are bureaucratic jargon and phonetic whims. Nothing more. Going from Florida to Georgia is about as exciting as going from page 228 to page 229 in the phone directory. The countryside is beautiful. But the civilization that it hosts is not so beautiful. Efficient, yes, and neat, and nourishing; and all those things. But it makes a caveman of the Pleistocene Age like me soporific. I prefer Europe with its irresponsible dogs that pee in the streets, with its different regions, with its brusque changes in citizenry. But I recognize the fact that uniformity fosters civilization and diversity tends to destroy it. The Yankees with their flawless epidermis and unicellular tissue have a tremendous inner strength.

And they are exporting it. By exercising spiritual leadership as a world power and through their multinational companies, these gentlemen are creating a world in their own image. This phenomenon is good for civilization but bad for individual nations. Good for the species but bad for the individual. Like Christianity, which swept away the pagan gods and eradicated the rich religious fantasy of the European peoples but at the same time brought them together through worship of a common mythology. Like Latin, which eradicated hundreds of languages and dialects impoverishing the lists of languages but making it possible for Virgil's little ditties to become known in an unprecedentedly large area of the globe.

No less important--as we shall see if an atomic blast doesn't prove me wrong--is Yankee cohesiveness. Little by little the world is becoming Americanized; everyone included--even the most vociferous anti-Yankees. The Coca-Cola plant which the poor Russians recently authorized is a cultural breakthrough. It's today's Cistercian monastery. It's the abbey on the frontier that converts the barbarians to Christianity. The hamburger is the creed that everyone will eventually know by heart. Freeways with their green signs and their cloverleaves are copies of Yankee models. So are fiber-glass skyscrapers, marketing techniques, and the businesslike way of commercial correspondence.

The main difference between the cohesive work of the Yankees and that of Rome or Christianity is that the Yankee model is carried out on a planetary scale. There are no heretics in their cultural realm. No distinctions are made. On the list are Russians, Indians and Argentineans. In addition, it's not a colonization by force, but voluntary, based on an axiom which admits no appeals: everyone imitates the leader-nation. And if we don't imitate, we are left by the wayside. It's as simple as that. Everything is becoming Americanized. The organization of the army, medical practice, fashions, sports, and topics of conversation. There's nothing more moving than watching a communist wearing blue jeans smoke a Marlboro and at the same time recite Marcuse and condemn the consumer society. Even anti-Americanism is a typically American product. When Brezhnev accepted a Lincoln as a gift, he fell into the trap, in the inevitable trap, because no one would ever dream of longing for a Volga or a Skoda. We dream of

Cadillacs because our dreams are American. In technicolor, to boot.

The phenomenon of the Yankee overflow, or looking at it from another angle, the phenomenon of acculturation toward the American model, has been made possible by a sacred book. Be it the Talmud, the Bible, or the Koran, a book is always indispensable. The Yankees also have one. It's called the Manual of Procedures. This book is inescapable. Every activity carried out by these gentlemen has its beginning in a manual of procedures. Every initiative, to be completely accepted, must be able to create a modus operandi that is easily transmitted and learned. War, love, a business contract, everything, absolutely everything, is written or will be written in a system. The system is implacable. It always works. It leaves nothing to chance. And it's within everyone's reach.

The US systematizes everything. It modifies and makes everything uniform. Everything is reduced to systems that later on are repeated, improved, and modified, but they never lose their capacity to create.

How long will the complete Americanization of the planet take? Well, I'm not Alexis de Tocqueville and can't answer that question. I'm not even Herman Kahn. But I imagine it will take less time than it took the Romans. Julius Caesar didn't have computers, and St. Peter was unfamiliar with commnication via satellite. The Yankees are playing with a stacked deck. Now, is this good or bad? Was the Christianization of the world a good thing? I don't know. Making value judgments of this kind puts you on shaky ground. If it's not gross superstition to believe that equality among men and nations is beneficial, I presume that any centripetal force at work in history is advantageous for the human animal. It ends up being positive. Positive for the species, which would make all bipeds favoring human solidarity happy, but which would dissatisfy the individualists. Personally I don't know where I stand. On Mondays, Wednesdays, and Fridays I'm a rabid Darwinist. On Tuesdays, Thursdays, and Saturdays, Spencerian. On Sundays I don't give a damn about anything. So for the time being everyone should think for himself and draw his own conclusions. Maybe some day they will give us problems that have alreay been solved. How long will it be before Spain is Americanized?

THE AMERICANIZATION OF MADRID

Madrid--topic and typical of the zarzuela[2]. The Madrid of Agustín Lara[3] who carpeted the Gran Viá[4] with carnations and crowned empresses in Lavapies[5]. This image of Spain created by Lara is still the one held by many Latin Americans. All that is long gone. The dandy sporting his beret and scarf with his little bit of daring and wit-- kaputt. The caterpillar of progress flattened him long ago. You can't be a Don Juan and operate out of an apartment on the floor above a Kentucky Fried Chicken joint. It simply doesn't work. Were there ever flower vendors? Those girls now work at Sears. And that rite of bathing someone in sherry-- I always did think it was a monstrosity. Well, nowadays the ablution would be Coca-Cola.

Spain, like Europe, like the Orient--especially the Orient-- is becoming Americanized. They are all following in the footsteps of the Yankees. What's in fashion today in San Francisco or New York, tomorrow will be in fashion in Paris, and day after tomorrow in Prague. The Americans determine the norms. Friends and enemies imitate them. When they make a breakthrough in the peaceful use of atomic energy, the Spaniards and Brazilians immediately get in the act and buy their cyclotrons. When American students discover the pleasures of smoking marijuana, their Dutch and German counterparts follow suit and light up a joint. An astounding Hamelinesque civilization. Behind their flutes we all march enchanted.

I imagine it's always been the same. The only difference now is that electronics, the mass media, and the irreverent concupiscence of our time give supersonic speed to what we call acculturation. Up until now, being able to discover the influence of one nation on another was a magical feat. Now it is a matter of opening your eyes. The age old adage has changed: the nations lagging behind run poorly because those out ahead run well. And way out ahead by a long distance is Uncle Sam wearing his olympic stars and stipes. When old timers return to Madrid, they scarcely recognize the place. They don't even see any madrileños[6]. Because of the continuous arrival of people from Asturias, Galicia and Andalusia, madrileños, like the manatee, are becoming extinct. They are an endangered species. They are accused of being lazy, revelers, easygoing (the old timers used to say to hell with it all). It seems that in all times and in all places mankind has found it amusing (when really it's stupid) to make generalizations. Following this hallowed tradition, the regions of Spain have branded the madrileños as lazy dandies. It's still unknown whether the generalization came before the bias or vice versa. But this is a serious matter best left to the experts.

Getting back to what I was saying--the American way of life has taken the Hispanic fortress by force (to put it in military terminology which would please the Spaniards since they have an epic concept of history). A Spanish-American tourist with his hands between his legs and a certain look of discomfort on his sweaty face who asks where the restroom is will be told that the "water closet" is to the left or under the stairs or next to the lady wearing the ridiculous hat. If you're in a taxi, the driver might tell you there's a traffic jam because it's the "rush." Now they're even talking about changing the work schedule--adjusting the clock to the American system. They're even talking about--God forbid--doing away with the siesta and closing the factories at 6 PM. Fat women are beginning to substitute Metrecal for their fabada[7]; sugar-free foods for potatoes. Spaniards feel a certain amount of pride because their average height has increased 2 centimeters, and the average weight has been reduced by a few grams. Cholesterol and pollution are now public enemies number one. The Americans inject us with their own neuroses, and their fads are contagious. The Celtiberian is being contaminated with the American aversion to an ample waist line--an aversion which has gotten all out of proportion. The Spanish figure is becoming taller, more slender, and lighter colored. The typical Andalusian who is short, fat, and dark and speaks with his own peculiar accent is almost a national disgrace. Rock and roll has wiped out the paso doble[8]. All the young singing groups cruelly butcher the English language with their strongly trilled r's. And the blues linger forever on the "hit parade."

When it comes to acculturation--just like anything else--you have to be pragmatic. It's inevitable. You try to patch up the cultural cracks to keep out foreign influence and end up annoying everyone. After all, if Americans don't eat morcillas[9], it's because it never crossed Edison's mind to be born in a nice Manchegan village. It's some consolation to know that he wasn't born in Tusiyamacho or Marseilles either. The whole world marches just as seriously as can be to the Yankee beat. There's no doubt about it. Spain is right in there, too. She doesn't miss a step. She can't even distinguish between what is genuinely American and what Americans have borrowed from other cultures and then exported. Perhaps the best example of this is the shabby interest in Oriental religions that Spaniards and Latin Americans are beginning to imitate.

AMERICANIZATION MADE IN THE ORIENT

We've got to be careful. India is exporting its holy men at an unusually fast pace. The invasion enters via California. It's always the Gringos. First it was a chubby kid--the Maharishi--and then a venerable old man. They all hold the secret to spiritual tranquility except when they arrive in the United States. Then everything becomes a business or it disappears. In a poor section of New York I once came across a neon sign which said "God, Inc." It was a modest church belonging to an industrious minister of one of the 14,000 religious sects in that country. He wasn't being irreverent, only honest and sincere. The same thing happens to the Indian holy men. To be successful in America you need a public relations man, two accountants, an advertising agency, a lawyer, malpractice insurance, a survey of marketing potential, and a speech writer. Next, a manager who coordinates the prophet's activities and a board of directors to approve the campaign. If the holy man is talented, he will end up with his shares being quoted on the stock market. If Siddhartha were to see this, he'd die of heart failure. But that's how the United States is. A Wall Street style magician who changes everything she touches into a business. The chubby kid that was the bearer of peace ended up with an ulcer. In underdeveloped India you can reach perfection without complications while lying in a street in Bombay under the haught gaze of the cows. In the United States all this becomes a hassle involving taxes, organization, a manual of procedures. In the end we face gastritis and cardiac arrest. There's no escape! Getting back to my point, India has exported the business of spiritual peace to the United States and the Gringos have decided to invest in it. For some years now almost everyone has been aspiring to reach nirvana. Perhaps what it really is is a subtle means of avoiding a heart attack. Nobody knows for sure. The Yankees have an obsession for electrocardiograms. The prankster who shouts "cholesterol" in a New York theater will have people jumping out of windows. Their fear is atrocious. The sad part is that those neuroses are contagious. The Spanish middle class and the Latin American intelligentsia--the two sectors that depend most on the United States--will end up becoming easternized by this American brand of decaffeinated Hinduism. Then the United States will come up with a brand-new neurosis as they did with the hallucinogens, and we'll go right on with the same old thing like a bunch of fools. It seems that one of the secret means of obtaining spiritual peace is transcendental meditation. You sit cross-legged--not me because I can't--close your eyes and wait for your chakra to open. Twenty minutes a day is all it takes. You shouldn't do it very late in the afternoon because the meditator--is that how you say it?--will receive too much energy. There is a proliferation of schools of meditation. The most advanced disciples are able to identify up to ten stages of meditation, more or less like St. Teresa--a maharishi in her day--who experienced seven stages on her trajectory toward union with God. The meditators, to be truthful, don't experience anything. Pure charlatanry of people living with illusions, but if that kind of activity makes them happy, fine. That's what it's all about. One does not <u>have</u> peace, war, or spiritual happiness; <u>he thinks he has</u> one or the other. That's all it takes. As for me, I prefer Sabu's India. I'll stick with the child who leads the elephant and not the chubby little mystic. I'm more interested in Kipling than Siddhartha Gautama. In other words, the only transcendental meditation is the one that fills our heads with ideas. To make your mind blank and say that you are meditating is a contradiction. To meditate is to have your mind seething with ideas, to worry, invent and create. Spiritual peace--the sweet and passive gentleness of these holy men--is a form of desertion. That is the least transcendental form of meditation since it doesn't go beyond simple rest. As such--as rest--it's acceptable, but please don't make pretenses about it's being something else even if it does come riding on a magic carpet or packaged up in the contradictory prestige of the Americans. This false orientalism brought to us via the United States that we are currently imitating is the clearest proof of our cultural weakness. All the Americans have to do is come out with an idea--even if it's as ridiculous as transcendental meditation -- for us to unhesitatingly ape them. Our creative big bang hasn't yet begun.

THE BIG BANG THAT HASN'T YET BEGUN

The tail--as everyone knows--dwells in the most unpleasant part of the animal. Its purpose is limited--almost always--to slaying insects. Its function hardly goes beyond that. It's that henchman which certain animals possess to keep law and order within their own individual geography. The comparison of a lion's tail to a mouse's head has given rise to the erroneous metaphor we use when we have no choice in a particular situation: if we have no alternative to being pulled along by the tug boat of the powerful, it's preferable to be the lion's tail. If we are left behind, then the only recourse we have is to be the mouse's head. As a matter of fact, both alternatives are unacceptable because the only good and viable option is to be the lion's head. The rest is rhetoric.

You don't need to be too bright to see how this fable applies to Spain and Latin America. Our ills stem from the fact that we have accepted being the lion's tail. Our nations fail to establish their own objectives. We are content to sail with the wind and follow in the wake of the big powers. At times, like now, new ways seemingly committed to solving our problems do appear--for example, the unsuccessful one in Chile and the ones in Cuba and Brazil. But unfortunately, they come to naught. These new paths lead to nowhere.

Our fundamental problem, the one that devours us, is not a lack of wealth and the fact that it is ill distributed, facts no one would dispute, but that our system of values, our models, our plans for development--in other words, the points of reference that we use to determine our cultural coordinates--are alien to our world. Philosophers and charlatans (who are more or less one and the same) call this phenomenon alienation. It's little consolation to know that nine tenths of the world's population is alienated if compared with New York (or London or Moscow), and that among those who are not alienated we find a few groups such as the aborigines of Australia and the Motilones Indians of Venezuela. In other words, even though England unleashed the Industrial Revolution over 100 years ago, up until now we have been unable to become participants in this craze, and now the Americans are already injecting us with the germs of the post-industrial neurosis concerning environmental pollution and the rhetoric against further industrial development. With loyalty worthy of a greater cause, we, the alienated, grotesquely feign to be great nations. We are like mirrors that tardily reflect distorted images. Buffoons.

How can we escape the magnetic pull of the world powers? It's senseless to prohibit long hair and bourgeois books and jam the shortwave signals as Cuba did. Sheer stupidity! It's something like burning the sofa to avoid adultery. To ignore the countries that march at the front of civilization is to behave like the Motilones Indians and the aborigines. Besides it's useless. In the long run their influence penetrates the millions of ever-open pores and then acquires the irrestible prestige of the forbidden.

It's all very clear. The only way to cease being a subordinate is to become a leader. Spain and Latin America must find a place of importance in the leadership of Western affairs. In order to do that, they must understand the ground rules of the game: the "leader-nations" have reached the top levels because they have the ability to successfully modify raw materials (technology); because of the increasing velocity with which they have produced these changes; and because of their unflagging efforts to mold the future. As long as our future is designed by outsiders, our present will be miserable. It is irritating to know with obnoxious certainty that tomorrow's fashions, our new ideas, our social customs, all of our future culture, will be a distorted version of what's happening today in Los Angeles or New York.

To sever this detestable dependency--the source of our restlessness and rancor--we must set forth on a path of creativity. We must rid ourselves of the self-contempt that keeps us from being bold and innovative and begin setting forth examples and models. I'm convinced that our impediments are more psychological than material. It's criminal for countries like Spain, Mexico, Brazil, and Argentina which have tremendous artistic and scientific potential to play such a small role in determining what direction civilization takes. Where do the Chilean, Cuban or Brazilian routes lead, if at the end of the road-- supposing they do go somewhere--we discover that we haven't covered much ground and that the happiness we are seeking is still like the damned carrot in front of the donkey? There are already numerous adventures to which we have no access: the atom, space, intramolecular life. And in the future there will be more.

It may seem tragic--and it is--that thousands of children in Paraguay and San Salvador are undernourished, but it is no less tragic that in their wildest dreams they can never imagine becoming an astronaut. For a Motilones Indian, an outsider in our culture, this is no big deal, but for us it's a brutal and devastating fact. Our politicians who are committed to the worthwhile struggle of reforming our social and economic structures must not forget the most important and urgent matter of all: reconstructing everyone's mentality, starting with themselves, which has become rusted by the rhetoric and short-sightedness of their office. Perhaps the slogan used by the "divine gauche" in Paris in May of 1968 should be made mandatory in our countries: "Power to the imaginative." To be truthful, those with imagination have always been in power in France. The roles played by de Gaulle--his defense at all costs of the greatness of France to avoid her becoming an appendix of the superpowers--is a magnificent example of the protean imagination of the old hero. Where imagination is really needed, direly needed, is in our poor and self-degraded Latin America. It is needed to free us from being either the lion's tail or the mouse's head. We need imagination to become something more meritorious and constructive which would prevent us from being mere passive objects of history written by others.

LATIN AMERICA AND SPAIN, NON-PARTICIPANTS IN HISTORY?

We Hispanic Americans--and with us nine-tenths of the world's population-- are on the verge of fading from the historical scene. Very soon the gap between the American scientific world and Argentina's or Chile's will be the same as the one between a Guajiro Indian of rural Venezuela and a citizen of Caracas. Unamuno's cry of "have them create" is an absurdity with a capital A.

Belonging to a community of nations--I do hope this is not too eloquent-- which is linked more or less to the Western Civilized World is almost a joke when you look at it from our impoverished and underdeveloped nook. The atomic age, in a sense, is already over. We scarcely heard of it in Latin America. The Space Age, which had it's beginning twenty years ago, is even farther out of our reach than the atomic one.

And there is already some indication that the future will be called the "genetic age." Man, but of course not the Latin Americans, will begin to manipulate life. He will create life, he will perfect it, he will modify it for his own benefit. We will continue to be spectators. We will bargain as our meager purse permits for an occasional scrap that falls from those laboratories, and more and more we will feel a confusing and basically unjust sense of inferiority.

The Papuans of New Guinea don't worry about not understanding the mystery of aviation, but aviation belongs to a world that has nothing to do with the Papuans. We can't renounce our world, but we are renouncing our role in history. Sometime toward the end of the 20th century, the curtain will be drawn between us and the Americans. We will live in two totally different eras even though we will still be inhabitants of the same planet. It's not a matter of our inferiority or their superiority. Stupidity of that sort died with Hitler.

What is really happening is that American industry, technology, science, and finances are closely meshed and aimed in one direction: toward progress. Their machinery moves at a tremendous speed which in turn generates even more vigorous impulses. If we add to this uncontrollable force the computer revoltion--an area in which Americans have attained prominence--we will have some idea of what the immediate future of that great nation will be.

The Russians will also be on the other side of the curtain. The Soviet industrial-scientific-financial complex doesn't have enough oxygen to keep up with the furious American pace. They are already suffering from shortness of breath, and they know it. To continue in the race, they have had to cast aside the burden of Marxism, but have retained the Leninist formula for political control. The price they would have to pay to catch up with the Americans would be very high: dismantle the bureaucracy created by sixty years of Communist Party control, ignore the reflexes of dogmatic thought, and trust more in the individual's effort to create a future mutually beneficial to all. Is that all? Just the demise of the Communist Utopia.

What can we Latin Americans do to become a part of this world that will eventually crush us? First, we must understand the problem in all its complexities and the risks involved. Second, we must react rationally, not emotionally. To start hating Americans hysterically, besides being very unfair, would cause us to fall further behind. Here it wouldn't be a bad idea to reiterate something that's already been said. The Americans don't owe their economic progress to our economic underdevelopment, but to their own economic rationale. If all the American property in Latin America were destroyed tomorrow, the United States would have lost a fraction of 1% of her gross national product (one trillion: a one and 12 zeros).

On the contrary, Latin America should profit from this phenomenon as cleverly as possible. The overabundance of capital and the expansionistic trend of American industry should be sources for our progress. There's no alternative. Our capitalists, our governments, our unions must learn the inner workings of neo-capitalism. Communism is an unacceptable model not only because of ethics but because of the undeniable fact that the communist countries also trail behind the great American super-power. It's the United States and not Russia that shapes everyone's world. Either we participate in the shaping of the world, in designing the future, or we are destined to slavishly imitate them.

The system worked for the Americans, and it will render the same results to those who know how to avail themselves of it. To understand this phenomenon and to profit from it, we must put aside our rancor, demagogic slogans and political provincialism. Perhaps there's still time to get aboard the first world.

NOTES

[1] Rubén Darió (1867-1916). Nicaraguan writer and poet; most important figure of modernismo.

[2] Zarzuela Light musical dramatic performance.

[3] Agustín Lara. 20th century Mexican composer, author of many famous songs well-known throughout Spain and Latin America.

[4] Gran Viá. Popular name for José Antonio Street in the heart of the old commercial district of Madrid.

[5] Lavapiés. An old picturesque district near the Plaza Mayor in Madrid.

[6] Madrileño. A native of Madrid.

[7] Fabada. A thick stew of white beans and sausages.

[8] Paso doble. A march rhythm typical of music associated with the bullfight.

[9] Morcilla. A kind of Spanish sausage.

II

THE US MODEL

IN THE BEGINNING WAS FREE ENTERPRISE

All for one and one for all. Have no fear. I'm not going to make a plug for the three musketeers. I'm going to try to explain why the USA is the greatest power on earth. Some hothead might say it's because they rob the underdeveloped nations of their wealth, but too much heat in the head usually causes our glorious thermocephalous colleagues' brains to evaporate. That's not the reason. It's just the opposite. The most wealthy nations are the ones that have a greater amount of commerce and business with the United States. This is easy to prove. Within reach of any biped capable of reading are the reports issued by the World Bank. The thermocephalic hypothesis is a perverse imbecility.

The "secret" of American power, it seems to me, is this: the society is made up of components which--far from struggling among themselves and presenting each other with obstacles--work together to strengthen free enterprise. Free enterprise is the backbone of the system. The universities graduate professionals for industry and commerce; the unions fight for concrete salary increases, optimum working conditions, and a bigger slice of the profit, but renounce the superstition regarding class struggles; the governnment tacitly or explicitly recognizes that "what's good for General Motors is good for the country." It's not a matter of a shameless surrender to capitalism, but a candid recognition that the economic organization of a country demands that, as a basic principle, all the working components function harmoniously together to obtain similar goals. Private companies, on the other hand, recognize that they have other responsibilities besides distributing dividends among their stockholders. Private companies conduct research and expand and create wealth. Their own internal dynamics compel constant expansion and modification. It's the heart of the system and its dialectic motor.

Seen from this angle, certain facets that at first seem strange suddenly become clear to us Latin Americans and Spaniards who are constantly at each other's throats. For example, the lobby. The lobbyists are people who publicly and openly defend in political circles certain economic interests. It's not dirty or covert. They are legitimate ambassadors from private enterprise sent to negotiate with the lawmakers. They exert pressure because pressure is one of the rules of the game. Bribing legislators is not part of the game--and there are numerous individuals who have ended up in jail--but defending the interests of those whom they represent indeed is.

The CIA, for example, recruits its agents--spies, analysts, and other similar species--from among the best universities. Just like Ford Motor Company, the Department of State, or the Army. Instinctively all of them consider themselves to be a part of the nation. Unions, entrepreneurs, public servants, policemen, and students are not separate classes in conflict with each other but parts of the same mechanism. The political parties don't attempt to destroy the system but to perfect it. The unions are not interested in crippling industry by using devastating strikes but try to obtain maximum benefits for their members. Students prepare themselves to become a part of their imperfect society and to modify it, but they have no intention of destroying it.

This mechanism, more problematic at times than at others, has been working for two centuries. Do you understand now why the United States is number one? It's true that its size (a little larger than Brazil), its population (4 times smaller than China's), and its natural resources (less than the Soviet's) provide potentiality for power. But it's obvious that the economic development of a nation is fundamentally a matter of cultural values. Japan, which is poor, small, and overpopulated, is making faster progress than any other country for the same reasons that made the United States great. Argentina, with ample space, capable labor and adequate infrastructure fails miserably at the task of becoming developed.

This brings up the moral question in the matter. Is it right for free enterprise to be the center of a social organization? The response must be qualified. Yes, it is right in a society that has subscribed to the values of success and profit and competition as a means of obtaining them. If the communists hold that the omnipotent party is the best vehicle for determining the success of their society, it's because they believe that the party can create more wealth and distribute it better. If some socialists hold that the unions should govern society, it's for similar reasons. Yankee capitalism organizes society around free enterprise. The real truth, not the one postulated by sacred books, but the other, the indubitable one, is that until now free enterprise has been more efficient than the party, the unions, or fascist corporalist entities in creating wealth and in its quantitative distribution. That's quite evident.

AMERICAN POLITICS

Dictionaries usually don't commit themselves: democracy is the government of the majority. But how that majority is counted is a horse of another color. We'll deal with that later on. Let's start by saying that the only absolute value capable of replacing monarchy was arithmetic. The king ruled by divine right without appeal. God so willed it. The English still ask Him to protect the monarch: God Save the Queen. As long as the royal will was revered because of its quasi-divinity, political order was coherent. The unquestionable authority of God backed the king. The real dilemma was how to substitute an equally unquestionable entity for the monarch without having recourse to theology. It was at that point that the arithmetic cult emerged, and the British motto became a laconic "In God we trust." A remarkable lesson. Once the superhuman powers are discarded no other absolute value remains except arithmetic. Three will always be greater than two and less than four. If we agree to accept the leadership of the majority, we are trusting in a system as legitimate as monarchy. Every human relationship that has no mathematical base will always be arbitrary and subjective. One can affirm that socialism is better than free enterprise or vice versa. One can argue that the liberals are more useful than the conservatives, or we can argue the opposite. But there's no biped outside an insane asylum who doubts the quantitative superiority of fourteen over thirteen. This simple reality is the essence of the metaphysics of democracy. It's not, of course, the suspicion that most people act wisely most of the time, but the melancholy conviction that by accepting a universal rule that is objective and without appeal people can work out their differences without the use of violence.

American politics stem from this pragmatic concept of democracy. That's why the two more or less similar political parties pass the power back and forth intermittently. The Democratic and Republican Parties are simply means of organizing the arithmetic equation without serious struggle. They are channels for coming to power with order.

The American politician emphasizes this pragmatism when practicing his profession. He relies on certain gentlemen, experts in public opinion polls, to reveal what issues interest the electorate. Then some sociologists will classify the electorate according to affinities, and a speech writer will prepare a speech aimed at flattering the ears of the potential voter. It all boils down to getting the individual to drop his ballot in the right box and having the god of arithmetic work things out in his favor.

Cynicism? On the contrary, it's pragmatism and a lack of ideological commitment. For Europeans and Latin Americans this is difficult to understand. The politicians don't want to change or reform the system. What they want is to <u>perfect</u> it. Except for certain insignificant mini-groups the political spectrum of the United States is practically monochromatic. The differences between a conservative and a liberal are pale and purely formal. The liberals subscribe to a certain central federalism while the conservatives lean toward greater local control. The liberals are in favor of vast public spending and a moderate social welfare program while the conservatives advocate that public benefits be reduced to a minimum and that each individual work out his own destiny according to his instincts and ability to work. In fact, the liberals and conservatives simply argue the amount and use of the national budget but without bickering about political options foreign to the system.

To point out more clearly the ideological uniformity of the American people and its political parties, both the Democrats and the Republicans have in their rank and file liberals and conservatives. There have been liberals (Rockefeller) among the Republicans and conservatives (Wallace) among the Democrats. If the blue collar workers and those in the lower income bracket lean toward the Democrats, it's not due to any class consciousness but to the indisputable fact that there are more liberal elements among the Democrats than among the Republicans and, because of that, during Democratic administrations a bigger slice of public spending usually benefits the less powerful.

This lack of disparate political options clearly reflects the socially uniform nature of the American people. The middle class comprises an enormous percentage of the population. A political party that exclusively represents the interests of the wealthy class or the very poor cannot exist since it would be swept away in any election. In spite of the fact that big business seems to get along better with the Republicans than with the Democrats, the Republicans are careful to nominate men (Eisenhower) who appeal to that vast and powerful middle class. On the other hand, there are no extreme positions which impede the effectiveness of a congress in which the majority belongs to one party while the executive power is affiliated with the other. There is always room for compromise when the issue being debated is of secondary importance. When it comes to basics, the Tyrians and the Trojans are of one accord.

Why haven't ideologies penetrated the American epidermis? There is no greater error than classifying the American conservatives as fascists or the liberals as Marxists. Fascism and communism are two ideologies totally foreign to American soil. And if their attempts to recruit have failed, it's due to the very obvious and evident reason that capitalism, in that country, has worked efficiently. Communism and fascism emerge as means for correcting capitalism. As substitutes for capitalism they have failed or become obsolete. But in the United States not only did capitalism not fail, it developed into a dialectic mechanism much more complex and efficient than what Marx could foresee. A protean system that has enabled it to reach a level of prosperity heretofore unknown in the written history of mankind. That prosperity has continued to flourish, and the system has prevailed over periodic crises which it has had to face. Why resort to another formula if the present one is producing splendid results? Americans believe in their economic system and their political order. As long as an uncontrollable crisis doesn't undermine the system, American Democracy will continue to be a simple struggle for the arithmetical majority. Perhaps this seems like a futile game in the politicized eyes of Europeans and Latin Americans, but no one can deny that it has produced positive results. The United States doesn't need statesmen like de Gaulle or Churchill. They can make do with Eisenhower, Truman, or Ford. The monolithic structure can endure the burden of mediocrity without risks. The most powerful man in the world--the president of the United States-- is a prisoner of a liberal capitalistic system that doesn't give him room for ideological adventures alien to the national idiosyncrasies. The electoral arithmetic would not allow him to do so. The future of the country is not at stake every time there is an election. There are no crises like those in France or Italy where not only the payrolls of the political bosses are at stake but also the very social structure of the country, its future prosperity and even its domestic tranquility. The mere fact that during an election the fundamentals of the system are not even debated helps reinforce it. A panic similar to the one that occurred among foreign and Chilean financiers when faced with Allende's election does not occur in the United States even when they are faced with the possible election of the most liberal candidate of the American political spectrum. Everything changes so that things may go on as usual.

A LESSON ON GRINGO ELECTIONS

It's a fact. Less than 50% of the Gringos turn out for elections. Not very good. But it is good that at the local level they vote on such serious issues as taxes, whether or not homosexuals should be allowed to teach in the school system, whether idiots should be allowed to spend enormous amounts of money exchanging colored chips in casinos, whether the firemen should purchase a new pump, or whether the police should begin using mercifully padded clubs. Electing Mr. Smith to represent us in Congress is always an inevitable mathematical procedure, even if unfortunately remote and somewhat akin to Brechtian alienation because their honors--the deputies, congressmen, senators, representatives of all different kinds of parliaments--are always so far away playing some kind of weird game-- politics--reaching a consensus in hallways and restaurants, an activity that is supposed to be the essence of the democratic process, but one that leaves us cold.

When democracy became representative, when it abandoned the assembly because there was no way to keep order among the multitude spilling over the plaza, it lost a great deal of its emotional effectiveness. Delegating is a minor evil, but it is an evil. The important thing is to be able to shout personally. To be there in the flesh when it's time to make decisions that affect us. To raise our own hands in person when it's time to count the votes.

Of course, our daily lives are directly affected by the issues of gambling, firemen, homosexuals, heterosexuals, the police, taxes, etc., etc.

The ideal situation would be to ask everyone personally his or her opinion on everything. And that ideal situation will perhaps come from a source we least suspected: science. The computer and the telephone, together, until a blackout separates them, can provide us with the most fantastic form of participatory democracy. There are small Yankee towns where they have installed systems for instantly polling public opinion. You can pick up the phone and express an opinion about whether they should build another basketball court instead of a municipal pool or whether the mayor is so stupid that he shouldn't be allowed to continue in office.

If George Orwell had had any notion of this new use of electronic computers, 1984 would have been a poem in praise of democratic hope. "Big Brother," instead of spying on our anguished existences, would have been something like a benevolent programmer, a solicitous pollster of our opinions.

What do you prefer for Saturday's concert? A band, a choir or a country music group? And the answer, happily, is anything but country music. That's democracy.

THE AMERICAN UNIVERSITY

There are close to three thousand of them. They range from small colleges with 300 students to mastodons like state universities in New York, California, and Puerto Rico. The budget of any one of these institutions is bigger than the budget of some Central American countries. For the purposes of this book--which is not a Yankee vademcum --it's sufficient to point out three interesting aspects. First, the American university doesn't revolve around the classroom but around the library; second , the student is not rewarded for his memory but for his creativity and for the precision of the method used in his reseach; and third, and most important, the institution is linked to its social environment. The goal of these centers is not to polish the intellect of the ruling elite but to furnish adequate personnel for the social machinery. It's all but amazing how supply and demand is reflected in the student's preferences. During the 50's there was an overflow of students in the sciences, in the 60's the humanities took on a glowing prestige, and in the 70's once again the trend is toward scientific careers. In a country linked to an incredible degree to the fluctuations of the market, it is appropriate for the cultural "stock market" to reflect the ups and downs of the economy. This may not seem too poetic, but unquestionably it is wise and practical. Especially for us Hispanics who are very familiar with university fauna more often useless than not.

Nowadays, as a general rule, the American university is not elitist. In order to be admitted to the best universities, you have to possess a good academic record, which allows them to maintain quality not only in the sciences but also in the area of humanistic knowledge which is more alien to American culture. It verges on embarrassment to have to acknowledge that for studying Medieval Spanish Literature the best center is not in Madrid, Barcelona or Valencia, but in Wisconsin; and that if you expect to become an expert in Golden Age drama you must go to North Carolina. Texas, to a great extent, specializes in Spanish American literature, and it's in Pittsburgh and not in Havana where it's possible to study in depth contemporary Cuban history. In each field at least one center, and sometimes several, tries to attain a level of excellence.

The fact that the students don't use the university environment as a place to express their criticism of the system brings about a climate that is conducive to learning and research. It was only during the unpopular Vietnam War that a handful of big universities suffered from a climate of political unrest. But this ended with the war. The campuses have once again become a placid cultural oasis in the midst of the hurly-burly of American life. The intelligentsia continues to flow from Harvard, Berkeley, Yale, Fletcher, Chicago, Rice and other vital centers toward key positions in the country. It seems to me that this relationship between the intelligentsia and American society in general has saved the country a lot of trouble. Perhaps the best place to observe this cooperation among diverse sectors of the country is in the space program, where NASA has been able to integrate in a common undertaking thousands of technicians from the armed forces, the universities, and private enterprise. In other much more rigid countries, those activities have been entrusted to only one sector of the nation, the military, probably because they are societies fragmented into separate compartments which have only a minimum amount of communication among them. American society with all its components coordinated in a common direction, founded on a system whose essence no one challenges, possesses a solid advantage over the vast majority of nations which are perennially involved in struggles not only of class but of professions and ideologies. In America not even the military is different from the rest of the country. Let's take a look.

THE MYTH ABOUT THE PENTAGON

The most frequent accusation found in anti-American slogans is "Warmongers." The same concept is expressed as "Pentagonism," a term used by the Dominican Juan Bosch, a mediocre short story writer and a worse politician. President Eisenhower gave rise to this legend when he made his unfortunate statement about a military industrial complex. The real truth is that the American military carries little weight as far as the political life of the country is concerned. When one of them, Douglas MacArthur, tried to ignore civil authority--a unique case in modern American history--he suddenly found himself ruthlessly retired. The military-- I insist--has little input beyond the perimeter of its activities. There are no military men prominent in political parties by virtue of their profession. There are no professional military men in the Congress. A few can be found in the Executive Branch. Anyone who anticipates a military coup in the United States is a raving maniac. This is a fantasy which is the result of extrapolation based on our own reality. An American general has no more influence than a doctor or an insurance salesman. The only ostensible difference among the three is that the general earns less money.

I don't mean to imply that the military is ignored. They are heard but only concerning decisions that pertain to them. It's reasonable for them to discuss military options with the President--the Bay of Pigs, the missle crisis, Vietnam--but when it comes to appointing cabinet members, Supreme Court justices or political candidates, you can rest assured that they will not be consulted. In a country of specialist, these gentlemen carry out their own responsibilities with maximum discretion.

For the last few years the total subordination of the military to the legislative and executive powers has been evident. In exceedingly long Senate hearings the military has had to give account of its actions, justify the defense budget, and explain the failures that it has experienced. Some generals--including the legendary Westmoreland--have not even been successful in becoming an integral part of the political life of the country. The electorate rejected him. The United States is a profoundly and decidedly civilian nation totally under the control of the political parties.

Nevertheless, Ike--obviously I don't like Ike--pointed to the danger of a certain military industrial complex. What was he referring to? The old inept general thought that the pressures brought to bear by the arms industries and the Pentagon could end up influencing the country's politics. This reinforced a fundamental falsehood which has been reported as an article of faith by the anti-Yankee tribes; the one that maintains that war was a strategem used by military industries to get rich and a means for the capitalists to remain afloat during their more critical stages. In the first place, the famous "military industry" is a subsidiary of the big industries. They are affiliates of General Motors, GE, and General Dynamics--to mention only three from a list of hundreds--that build airplanes for civilian aviation as well as for the military. Tanks as well as cars. Contracts with the Pentagon, fat during war time, probably reinforce the financial gains of some affiliates, but no one doubts--and least of all the economists working for these giants-- that war, seen from a panoramic perspective, is counterproductive for the economy and by the same token for the giants themselves. It has become perfectly clear to the world that the bloody venture in Indochina provoked an inflationary crisis in the American economy that culminated with the devaluation of the dollar. It is now, in the midst of a tense climate of peace, that the American economy is beginning to recuperate, and even though the arms industry affiliates obtain fewer contracts, the greater part of civilian industry is improving ostensibly. It's a malicious lie to maintain that war is the business of capitalism. During the last few years, what wars have Switzerland, Sweden, Germany, or Japan fought to increase their capitalistic economies? There is no argument more pedestrian than the one that postulates that behind each historical event you can find economic factors almost exclusively. Among the pitiful consequences of Marxism perhaps none is more pathetic than the sterilization of certain minds when it comes to making an analysis. Can anyone seriously say that the Americans were defending a market in Indochina? The cost of two weeks of war tripled the hypothetical advantages of a decade of exploitation. Does anyone really believe that Hitler's concept of *Lebensraum* justifies World War II? Or what calculated economic intentions sent 15,000 Cubans to Angola? Or is it that these secret economic factors apply only to capitalism? Vietnam is not, of course, the best example of a war whose purpose was one of economic exploitation. It's obvious that it was sheer stupidity. There's no doubt that American participation reached the point of genocide, but for me it's an absurd simplification to attribute it to a conspiracy among the Pentagon, Wall Street, and Big Business. That kind of explanation can only satisfy the most unimaginative.

The dreadful Pentagon is, after all, an extremely complex colossal structure that manages affairs of war with a certain degree of success, but by no stretch of the imagination does it control the nation. And it is important to keep in mind that Secretaries of Defense are civilians. Moreover, it's healthy for a substantial part of the academic training of the military to be given by the universities themselves. It's not unusual for military strategy to be publicly debated among university students and not in the privacy of the barracks. Kissinger, who has been the most significant figure for the military, was a professor at Harvard specializing in political-military strategy. The ex-Secretary of Defense, Melvin Laird, a civilian, was given his post for being an expert in options in the event of controlled nuclear war. The CIA, the *bête noire* soon to be discussed, has almost always been in civilian hands. And that's because the total separation of "civilian" and "military" is not manifest in the United States. The characteristics inherent in an open society--universities that mold officers enrolled in ROTC programs, the concept of public service shared by the military as well as the rest of the civil servants--all of these have narrowed the gap between the "civilians" and the "military." I'm not even sure that one can talk about "soldier mentality" in describing the stereotype of the American military man. Basically he is a citizen who carries out his own special job. No more, no less. The "Latin" military stereotype does not match his American counterpart. That rigid, authoritarian, patriotic, conservative individual has nothing in common with the American soldier. There is no appreciable difference between the social mentality of a colonel and that of a postmaster. They are one and the same; both little men. That mysterious centripetal force at work in one of the most homogeneous social structures in the world is present in the absence of a supposed military mentality. This certainly contributes to strengthening the system. Americans, unlike Latins, don't go to bed worrying about the possibility of waking up the next morning and finding a military government. This could happen only in the wildest of dreams. But what about the CIA? Let's take a look at it.

THE CIA: BETWEEN THE DEVIL AND THE DEEP BLUE SEA

Sooner or later every CIA has its Watergate just as every turkey has its Thanksgiving. This powerful agency is presently under the scrutiny of the courts, and it would not surprise me if a good number of its agents ended up behind bars. That's the risk you take when you play cops and robbers for such an extended amount of time. In the end, the roles become confused and it's hard to tell who's wearing the badge and who's wearing the mask. Especially in the United States. The United States is a Sadducean country, and it's fortunate that it's that way. Perhaps the greatest injustice in the New Testament lies in its severe treatment of the Sadducees and the Pharisees, fanatics, after all, concerned with the strict fulfillment of the law. But now we're talking about the CIA. In Spain and Latin America it's important for us to talk about the CIA because our lands were once the favorite haunts of James Bond; however, because of Watergate they won't be quite as popular now.

The Baby's Parents

The CIA was established in 1947. Keep this in mind. Before that date, the United States had militarily intervened in five Caribbean countries--Cuba, Panama, The Dominican Republic, Haiti, and Nicaragua. In addition, there were two interventions that occurred in Mexico. The first one greatly reduced her territory and the second one, termed a "punitive expedition," was directed against Pancho Villa. It's quite obvious that Allan Dulles' scheme wasn't the first example of Yankee intervention. In the long run what he really did was modify it and make it more subtle by keeping the American regular army from participating directly in the conflicts. It was only when the CIA found it impossible to manipulate certain political events in the Caribbean area that the United States army once again was called on to intervene (Dominican Republic, 1965).

Nevertheless, the CIA wasn't exactly the secular arm of American imperialism. This explanation is too simple and Manichean to be true. The CIA was the natural outgrowth of a political scheme brought about as a consequence of World War II. The United States saved Europe from the horrors of Nazi-Fascism and in its rescue operation resuscitated the Soviet Union, which since that time has been her obstinate enemy in a world fragmented into two irreconcilable factions. It's senseless to argue against the logical validity of the Washington vs. Moscow scheme; communism vs. anti-communism. Probably it was wrong (like all schemes), but until very recently it was the dogma on which preachers based their sermons. Each country of the "western bloc" thought of itself as a soldier of "Christian civilization" in the service of "the leader of the free world"; each country of the "eastern bloc," more or less the same, but on the opposite team. In this context the CIA emerged. At first it was an espionage operation, but after a while it became a catalytic agent for the interests of the "free world," as interpreted by Washington, of course. It was not a matter of strictly economic interest, as the Marxists with their habitual simplicity think, because in fact the greatest adventures of the CIA have taken place in areas of little economic importance or in areas where there were very weak commercial ties: Guatemala, the Congo, China, Vietnam, Indonesia, Iran, or Cuba. The losses suffered by the multinational cooperations in Cuba amounted to about one billion dollars, an amount they recovered without any difficulty by means of certain temporary tax exemptions signed by Kennedy. The manipulation of events in Iran date from 1953 when it was impossible to foresee the future economic importance of the Persians. No intelligent person can believe that only the protection of the Coca-Cola company--to use a caricature of my own--is responsible for the senseless and bloody intervention in Vietnam. There is another much more important factor: the American role. And I want to stress this point. In 1945 after the surrender of Japan and Germany, the United States assumed very seriously the role of world leader. This coronation had its beneficial consequences, for example the Marshall plan and the democratization of Germany and Japan, and its tragic sequels, for example Korea, Vietnam, and the CIA. If half the world accepted being embroiled in a life and death struggle with the communists and accepted the material and spiritual leadership of the United States, I think it's extremely dishonest for them to roll their eyes and pull their hair when they become aware of the activities of the CIA. They, like Sweden, should have rejected the CIA by renouncing the whole idea of the cold war but never forgetting its raison d'être. The CIA existed because the leader of the free world needed a "free-world" billy stick for nocturnal rounds, and everybody knows what billies are for.

The Ideological Ground Trembles

In 1959, with Cuba, the scheme of the two warring factions began to break up. This Antillean satellite--pardon my language (political jargon has a way of hanging around longer than it should)--defied the geographic rules of the conflict and spoiled one of its favorate axioms: the domino theory, which says that when one country falls under communist dictatorship, others in the same area follow suit. Cuba fell and nothing happened. She sent and was sent saboteurs. She received and sent out guerrillas. Now, finally exhausted, Washington and Havana are presently in a prenuptial phase, temporarily clouded by Cuban intervention in Angola. The axiom was false. There is a communist dictatorship ninety miles from the United States and nothing has happened (in the United States, I mean, because in Cuba it's another kettle of fish). The former French Congo is another example, and nothing happened there either. In other words, the policeman couldn't do his job and it really didn't matter. Espronceda,[1] who didn't have much of an imagination and was given to repetition, would have exclaimed "what does the world care that there is one cadaver more?"

The disappearance of the axiom will curtail the

activities of the CIA up to the limits of the new hypothesis. In all probability the perimeter of "the-free-world-that-must-be-defended" will be determined by its degree of development. The United States--it seems--will accept only being head of the "first world" team and then only if these countries themselves rather than the Americans maintain their own internal security.

The Vacuum Left by the CIA

Although the absence of the CIA is not exactly regrettable, its withdrawal will oblige the governments of Spain and Latin America to have a foreign policy for the first time. And it's high time. All that business of "let them run things" and even "let them spy" is all over. This new foreign policy should be well structured and should seek certain clearly defined objectives. The CIA did not limit its activities to anti-communist policing. When it could, it supported liberal efforts against military dictatorships. Don't forget the Congress for Cultural Freedom whose most outspoken defender was a, as matter of fact, Cuba's present Secretary of State, Raul Roa. Remember the periodicals Cuadernos Americanos and Nuevo Mundo. The latter under the capable leadership of Emir Rodríguez Monegal was a just and intelligent sounding board for the "Latin American boom." Remember the Dominican CIDES and the Instituto Democrático de Educación Política (Democratic Institute for Political Education) in Costa Rica. Remember the support of the CIA for the Spanish Congreso de Munich (Munich Convention) and its financial contributions to anti-Franco groups. It's well known that the personnel for the CIA has been recruited from liberal American universities, and consequently, the CIA is not only "anti" but also "pro." The stance was not a smoke screen but the logical policy of an organism that believed it was the sword and shield of a liberal democratic nation. When the activities of the unfortunate "Agency" are looked into in depth--and fortunately they will be looked into during the present hearings--we will see that these spies were infinitely more progressive and liberal than their cousins in the Department of State (another group that dances to the same tune).

What are the other democratic countries of the American hemisphere going to do? Someone will have to "eliminate" the Trujillos or support the Juan Bosches (and I mean Juan Bosch when he was Juan Bosch). If not, the rightist dictatorships, skillfully and shamelessly organized, can become masters of the continent. What are Venezuela, Colombia, Costa Rica, and Mexico going to do? I'm not suggesting Pan-American neo-interventionism but encouraging, internationally, groups with similar ideals. In Europe the social democrats and the Christian democrats coordinate their activities, and they help each other. The reproachable error of the CIA consists of making murky and obscure what could be and must be transparent. In Chile it would have been legitimate, reasonable, and correct for the American Democratic Party to have aided Frei's Democratic Christians or for the Republicans to have aided Mr. Alessandri's conservatives much in the same fashion that the Russian communist party did. American passion for cheap espionage and their dubitable mistake of involving the CIA in a matter that was beyond its jurisdiction led to the melodrama of an anonymous agent delivering mysterious envelopes in the cafes of Santiago, Chile.

There are already four international political organizations at work in Europe: the communists, the socialists, the Christian democrats, and the liberals. This is in keeping with the make-up of the European parliament and continental political strategy. In the Americas we should employ the same system since the parties are ideal channels for this kind of solidarity. And certainly police or espionage activities should not be used for this purpose. At the headquarters of Mario Soares' Portuguese socialist party I have seen English laborites and German social democrats offering their experience to that fledgling organization. If Latin-American progressive democrats wish to remain in power, they will have to resurrect the rusty internationalism of the democratic left. Amitore Fanfani has said that "if the CIA didn't exist, it would have to be invented." This Italian politician, with as much crudeness as common sense, is referring to the real dangers which threaten the system in which he believes. In Latin America strong arms tactics are a fact of life, and in Europe it's the KGB and the subordination of the enormous French and Italian communist parties to the dictates of Moscow. In spite of Berlinguer's strategic change in party lines, the communist parties are a kind of Soviet style CIA which are very difficult to ignore. Maybe the temperature of the cold war has decreased, but it's still a fact that fascists and communist make a conscious effort to undermine bourgeois democracies. I think it's great that these gentlemen with their hidden microphones and corrupt billfolds are hightailing it, but as biology has proved, necessity creates the organ. What is disappearing now is the organ; some of the necessities, unfortunately, are still around.

PROLETARIAT OF THE WORLD, UNITE

In the United States hunger has more followers than the Communist Party. Especially since a court of justice ruled that agents of the FBI secretly registered in the Communist Party must renounce their membership. Only Angela Davis and two or three other members are left. And for sure no labor leader belongs to the party because anticommunism in the United States is essentially proletarian. George Meany, president of the AFL-CIO, was the most consistent and strongest opponent of communism. London's Daily Telegraph on August 14, 1975, published an excellent article on the labor leader which explained his reasons for rejecting détente. No beating around the bush. Meany was anticommunist because no system in existence is worse for the worker than a dictatorship of the proletariat. This fact is understood not only by George Meany but by the two million Yugoslavian workers presently living and working in Switzerland and Germany. There must be some reason why out of hundreds of thousands of Spanish workers who emigrate in search of work not one goes to any of the proletarian paradises.

But Meany, besides being anticommunist, opposes détente. It's not true, he thinks, that it's the only alternative to war. Diplomatic and commercial ties are incapable of preventing a military conflict. He also recalls that in 1939 Germany was England's most important commercial partner. The one and only way to halt Soviet aggression is a well stocked arsenal and a finger on the trigger. Détente--in the opinion of the labor leader Meany--will serve only to stimulate Moscow's imperialistic appetite. He also believes that détente further aggravates things because in exchange for a dubious handshake the United States will cede technology, food, and resources that in the final analysis will only serve to strengthen the Soviet military machine which will then be better able to utilize a greater part of their budget.

Meany's opinion, without doubt full of American

common sense, contradicts Milovan Djilas' opinion. The author of <u>The New Class</u> thinks détente may be the downfall of communism since its superstitions will be swept away by the winds of freedom which Russo-American rapprochement brings with it. In order for the Yugoslav to be right, the Soviets, of course, will have to crack a window for that wind to come through. Whether this happens or not remains to be seen. The first indications have been negative. The Soviet Union still denies visas to western reporters and restricts the free circulation of men and ideas. That ruthless question that Lenin asked in 1920 is still brutally in force in the party's logic: "Freedom for what?"

European communists are usually perplexed by the militant anticommunism of the American unions. For example, it's possible for business deals made between friendly capitalists and smiling communists to go down the drain because American dock workers refuse to load the merchandise. American unions practice indisputable pragmatism rather than following dogmatic guidelines. Anything representing increased buying power and a reduction in physical labor is good for them. The opposite is bad. If the sale of wheat to the USSR raises food prices in the United States, its results are negative for the working class; therefore, they oppose it. The fact of the matter is that it's a much easier task to be an American union leader than a Soviet one bogged down in the dialectic jargon which demands that they work to produce more in order to consume less to build a strong nation.

The simple, efficient instinct of the American unions is based on two premises: first, the legitimacy of making a profit or gain as the ultimate reason for human initiative. There is nothing reproachable about people working to have more, be they capitalists or proletariat. It's perfectly moral to invest capital and earn dividends. Second, the Yankee unions have no desire to destroy the system that has served them so well. On the contrary, they want to use it, perfect it, and in exchange for their work receive their proletarian profit: increased purchasing power and less physical labor. At the same time they support fiscal legislation that channels a substantial part of the profits from the capital to the workers in the form of social programs. Moreover, the categories "capitalist" and "worker" are not rigid. The stockholders of big corporations are full of workers, and the class to which a salaried multi-national executive belongs is very difficult to define. American labor unions have not fallen into the Byzantine theology of class struggle.

Perhaps it's this attitude on the part of the Yankee proletariat that has made the nation great. Rather than kill the goose that lays the golden eggs, they pamper her and grease her ovaries. Apparently, there is no better way for a New York electrician to earn $13.50 an hour, send his son to college and have a big car to drive to Florida on his vacation. This image may seem grossly materialistic, but it's close to the paradise dreamed about by Polish workers. It's quite easy to invoke spiritual values when you're seated at a desk in the Communist Party's local headquarters. But the American worker doesn't swallow that kind of story.

THE SYSTEM IS PURGED

In Spain and Latin America we followed the gory details of Watergate with anticipation similar to that demonstrated by soap opera fans. And with certain disbelief, let's be honest. Since we're used to political trickery, bribe, espionage and abuse of power, it seemed incredible to us for the most powerful man in the world to be on the verge of being sent to jail for precisely that kind of activity. How can you convince a paranoiac leftist--one of those who sees the CIA or the FBI no matter where he looks--that those very institutions quake in their boots when any old Sirica beats on his desk with the gavel? I wonder what the idiot who believed that the American Congress was a branch of the Mafia thought when he found out that it harbors the highest concentration of puritans per square foot in the whole world. Or the other deluded soul hellbent on defining the American press as an instrument of big business. This time the Americans, who often set bad examples, have set a marvelous one. And we should imitate them in this instance just as we do when it comes to drinking coke and chewing gum.

Perhaps the secret of Saxon stability is rooted in the trust the English and the Americans have in the <u>system</u>. They really <u>believe</u> in their laws, in their legislatures, in their judges, in their elected officials and in the right each of these has to carry out his job. South of the Rio Grande--Spanish heritage--no one believes in anything. There is a sense of fatalism which takes for granted that the laws only serve to make a certain few wealthy; that the judges will be bribed by the powerful; and that the official that happens to be in power is a crook of the biggest sort.

Américo Castro[2] believes that this cynical and pessimistic attitude is the result of certain historical factors present in Spain during the Middle Ages, the period in which the Spanish character was formed. He maintains that this attitude results from difficulties encountered by the three diverse groups--Moors, Christians, Jews--living together and from the long submission of one group to another. The "system" was always an arbitrary straightjacket. Add to this the creole mistrust of the corrupt Spanish Colonial Administration and you have the skeptical and negative creature that grazes in our lands. No matter what the origins may be, their consequences are with us, alive and well. We had rather believe in UFO's than in the honesty of our political leaders.

And the worst part is that almost always we are right; frequently the men in the system are rotten. How can you change the age-old attitude of the homo hispanicus? I think the answer is obvious: with a dozen Watergates; with newspapers that expose matters forcefully; with judges who sentence high government officials, generals or supreme court justices; with officials who are incorruptible when faced with venality; with legislatures honest to a ridiculous extreme; with office holders who don't accept bribes. There is no other honest way of soliciting the loyalty of the citizenry to the system except by making everyone abide by the rules of the game. The government is a tool of the state and not vice versa. From the president of the nation down to the last mailman, all the power structure is no more than a chain of public servants subject to the immediate application of the law. How can an honest young person keep from looking down on the "system" when he knows in his country you go to jail for stealing a dozen shirts from a store and not for accepting a bribe from a dishonest contractor? Why would we expect patriotism and scrupulousness from the average citizen who observes how the rich man who breaks the tax laws of the country goes unpunished? But is it morally just to require the rich man to pay his taxes when it's unclear what the final destiny of those funds will be? The most urgent revolution needed in the Hispanic world is a moral one. There will be loyalty to the system when political vocation becomes a willingness to serve rather than a means of attaining power and personal gain; when failure to pay taxes becomes a despicable crime because it is robbing the nation; when the citizen is convinced that the law protects him from the criminal--be he thief, bishop, or policeman--and when the institutions are above the individual. Why are there only a handful of communists and fascists among the 220 million Americans? It's as simple as this: because Watergate is possible. Because in that country's jails there is space for everyone and not just a few. We who import everything from the Gringos should import as soon as possible these magnificent scandals. It's urgent. It's a matter of life and death.

IF THE EMPEROR IS NAKED

There was a time when God was a kind of employment agency. The hierarchies depended on His divine will. Those who ruled-- lamas, Incas, pharaohs, kings, and other creatures of royal ilk--were linked to the Creator no matter which of these omnipotent versions they happened to be. Before decapitating his fleeting client, it is said that the headsman who executed Charles I made a pathetic supplication: "Your highness, explain to God that I am just an instrument of those persons who are violating His will; be sure He doesn't get confused." Charles benevolently agreed to take the message.

Whether the anecdote is false or inexact is of little importance. What it really does is emphasize the divine character of the hierarchy and the terror that such origin caused among its subordinates. From those dark ages a fragile myth has survived: dignity of the office. Plebean democracy, far from ending this superstition, ended up subscribing to it. The president shouldn't be called a crook even if he is because of his office. A corrupt justice and an idiot professor are treated with kid gloves. The curule chair, the throne, the professional chair, and other royal seats give their occupants a mysterious aura of respect. The "office" that on one hand obliges the subordinates to be respectful, on the other subjugates the occupants, committing them to a certain seriousness which forces them to adopt certain attitudes, postures, and gestures befitting the office they hold.

It's a pity that students of body language haven't devoted themselves to classifying the repertoire of gestures of members of the hierarchy and their clearly atavistic condition. It increases according to the rank they hold. It runs from the lowliest bureaucrat with his ever present necktie to the Japanese Mikado, a living god in perpetual hieratic pose because the stability of the universe depended on his immobility.

But let's get down to brass tacks before this rambling ends up hiding the real purpose of these reflections. For months the Watergate affair haunted us. I believe that the most important aspect of the whole episode was the erroneous defense which was made for Richard Nixon. The most powerful defense in his favor was not that he was innocent but that "he was president." This is the same rationale that has been used for years in Spanish America to preserve the prestige of our healthy pack of political bosses. If a dishonest general is denounced, the "honor of the whole army is at stake." If the corruption of the chief executive is pointed out, "the presidency is degraded." It seems to me that all these interpretations are wrong. The office itself does not have dignity. Dignity is provided by the person who occupies the office. Once and for all we must annihilate this fetish. The office of the president, the general, the bishop, cabinet members, or professors is not blemished simply because the president, a general, a cabinet member, or a professor is exposed and proved to be stupid and dishonest. Nor are those offices strengthened because of the wisdom and honesty of those that occupy them. Dispensing with any kind of magic relationship between men is implicit in the spirit of democracy. Tom, Dick, or Harry should be in office because of their virtues, and if they turn out to be frauds, they should be told so and kicked out.

Watergate has been the best thing that could have happened to the United States in view of the growing loss of faith in the system prevalent among the youth. Confidence in that nation and in the vigor of its institutions is reborn when chiefs of police, cabinet members, and generals appear with trembling voices in the courts of justice. The law applies to everyone in that great country. It's untrue that it is weakening. It is gaining strength. The faith of its citizens in the press, in the judicial power, and in the legislative bodies is growing. The Vietnam war deserter knows that jail is not only for victims of the establishment but that if the establishment itself trespasses beyond certain limits it too will be implacably purged. The oppressed black discovers that to obtain justice you don't have to resort to wild riots because justice already exists, with all its defects, at the very core of the nation. The Watergate scandal has been a valuable experience. After knowing all the details of the episode, how can anyone who is intelligent say that the nation is in the hands of the CIA or the FBI or the Pentagon or the corporations? Hasn't everyone seen the CIA and the FBI and the White House in the judgment seat? Hasn't everyone seen the "press-bought-by-capitalism" goading the spinal column of the system (the corporations)? How can anyone with self-respect go on using those everyday clichés?

What saves that country, in the final analysis, is the merciless ferocity of its self-criticism. It has faults, to be sure, but they are aired in public; they are exposed and corrected. There are injustices, of course, but they are not hidden; they are discussed. If that is a symptom of decline, well then I'm all for it. At this time I don't believe there are many countries that could withstand the spectacle of seeing their president crushed by the weight of his wrongdoings. The Nixon episode did not damage the image of the presidency but the image of the man himself. This is an essential difference not perceived by those who still assume that the power structure has theological origins. As in the tale by Juan Manuel[3], if the emperor is naked, he must be told. The sooner, the better.

NOTES

[1] José de Espronceda (1800-1842). Famous Spanish Romantic poet. The phrase quoted is from the poem entitled "Canto a Teresa."

[2] Américo Castro (1885-1972). Spanish essayist, literary critic, and philosopher and author of *La realidad histórica de España*.

[3] Don Juan Manuel. Medieval Spanish author of moralizing tales.

III

REFLECTIONS ON IMPERIALISM AND DEVELOPMENT

CONSUMER SOCIETY: MYTH AND REALITY

Early in the sixties, the American sociologist Vance Packard lucidly deciphered what comprises the dialectic of progress in advanced capitalistic societies. Basically, Vance Packard's books were to prove that man of the "first world" was a *homo consumens*, a being condemned to work in order to acquire consumer goods for which advertising had diabolically "created" a prior need. Thus trapped between the psychological manipulators of advertising on one hand and the incessant flow of new gadgets on the other, our poor Sisyphus pushed the stone of toil up the hill without the remotest hope of arriving at the top; the top, of course, being the satisfaction that would justify his effort. Man saw himself bound by material things, a prisoner of gadgets, and a slave of tasks not justified by the possession of those goods; a situation which caused him to move in a meaningless circle. The term used to describe this man immersed in this pandemonium was "alienated" and the prophets beat their drums in his defense.

The Prophets Appear

In California, the German Marcuse shook his lion-like mane, put one foot on the books of Vance Packard, another on those of Freud, and another on those of Marx. For Marcuse it's not hard to have three feet. From Vance Packard he took his diagnosis concerning society; from Marx perhaps the only aspect that he remotely left intact was his theory about alienation in capitalistic societies; from Freud what no one takes seriously in his very serious and respectable mythology: the hypothesis that culture was the result of inhibitions of the libido. According to Marcuse, at our present stage of development, a society without inhibitions headed toward progress is indeed possible. In other words, Marcuse used Freud just so he could contradict him.

With a diagnosis like Vance Packard's and with a prophet at the head of the multitude, the trial against consumer society was organized at an international level. It had to be condemned, and a harrowing expression appeared on the faces of many people. The hippies accused consumer society as if it were Adolf Hitler and not as an abstract concept. The politicians--attuned to the times--incorporated into their tribunal gibberish attacks on affluent societies suffering from this horrible "consumerism." The principal culprit was the United States.

The Pure Unadulterated Truth

All this is a labyrinth of words. We have become lost in a sea of words and don't know how to emerge. That's the cause of our anguish and pessimism. There is no way of escaping from these prisons of words. It's not true that today's man is a prisoner of things. Man <u>is</u> his things. What man has been throughout his long period of evolution which goes back millions of years is what those "things" he has been creating have allowed him to be.

Human enterprise has always ridden on the shoulders of that interdependence. Movable type created the necessity for books just as the automatic washing machine created the need to wash clothes mechanically. Man's basic needs are food, rest, and sex. But as it turns out those basic "needs" are no different from those of the rest of the animals.

His secondary needs which developed over the centuries are precisely what confers on man that distinction that we want to grant him. Development , progress, can be defined as the accumulation of secondary needs. The reader can call them "alienators" if he wants to, but remember that Sartre, who meditated daily on the essence of Being, lived as alienated as John Doe, who works to acquire consumer goods. In the long run both spend their lives engaged in activities foreign to human beings.

Nowadays since the rhythm of life has aggravated the complexities of our culture and man has developed an infinite number of secondary needs, there is emerging a fear regarding the kinds of lives we are leading and a false nostalgia for more simple, less complex forms of life. All that fuss is unnecessary. It is false that our society is sick for reasons mentioned by Vance Packard. Things have never been different; it's just that the progress of our time comes at us with such tremendous speed that we tend to withdraw out of fear.

Homo consumens began to emerge with the discovery of fire, darts, and arrows or the invention of the wheel. There is no "alienation" today that has not previously existed. To be man is to be alienated. Alienated in some way, prisoner of some kind of system of dogmas or fetishes. As long as man fails to understand the meaning of existence--and he always will-- "to live" will be a phenomenon that will always take place under the cover of some kind of alienation.

All that extravagant literature that Marcuse and other minor prophets have put in circulation is very dangerous. It leads to an obsessive nihilism that assaults society without offering any reasonable alternatives. We know what they're against, but what they're *for* is still a secret. If for once they were to realize the emptiness of all nihilistic rhetoric, there is no doubt that they would abandon it. I hope this happens before the damage becomes irreparable.

The premise is absolutely necessary if we want to debate the topic of our development within the framework of our relationship with the United States and other countries of the so-called First World. Knowing the "why" of development is as important as knowing the means of obtaining it or knowing how to explain to ourselves why we haven't obtained it.

LAMENTS AND RECRIMINATIONS

If the meetings of UNCTAD have accomplished anything, it has been to utter a bloodcurdling cry when confronted with the poverty of the masses and the wealth of a few. That forum--plagued with demagogy, apocalyptic speeches, *mea culpas*, recriminations, and occasional nonsense--has loosened the angry bull of hunger in the ring and called for someone to fight it.

From the underdeveloped corner--an enormous corner that includes three-fourths of all the bipeds that ill graze on God's green earth--rose the strident voice of the prosecutor. It seems that the developed nations or the multinationals are to blame for our hunger, our illiterate populations, and our filthy children riddled with parasites. Or maybe it's the organizations that lend at high interest rates and sell at high prices and buy little. It seems that the rich countries are wealthy at our expense. No! This is not true. This is totally false. We ourselves--primordially we ourselves--burdened with several centuries of distorted structures are responsible for our misfortunes.

Why should Japan--emaciated by the bombs of World War II, smoldering and radioactive, starving and left without industry or arable land--blush because of her booming prosperity? What crime is involved in the inexhaustible industriousness of that nation or in the skillful handling of production-research marketing? The same could be said about Germany or Italy. Of what kind of colonialism can Switzerland be accused? Or Sweden? Or the United States? When will we who live south of the Rio Grande realize that the "fabulous" business that the United States has with Latin America comprises only a fraction of one percent of her gross national product? And if that country gave more orders than it received in Europe--and Europeans aren't defenseless-it's because its gigantic internal market, where even children are consumers, absorbs 90% of the production.

Why blame England for the millennial horrors of India, its castes, its maharajahs and the immunity of her cows? Why does it hurt us to admit that we have been unable to impose tax reforms that would better distribute the national income? Why aren't we ashamed of our universities that do no research, of our brains that do not invent, or of our industries that fail to innovate? In some of our countries there are politicians that sack the national treasury. And places where the word "politician" is synonymous with "crook." And where the unscientific demogogic agrarian reform replaces the unproductive Latifundio.[1] There are parcels of land in the Spanish world where the best plans slowly sink into bureaucratic quicksand. Or where the ignorant have power because they have some relative in office. Countries where talent is considered a dangerous crime. Who doesn't believe in the dirty tricks of some of the multinationals or in businesses in which each individual seeks personal gain? If Brazil could quadruple the price of coffee or Chile the price of copper or Bolivia the price of tin, who doubts, and rightly so, that they would bleed their neighbors? Cuba, for example, prospered during wartime. The Allies-her allies-- paid her more for sugar.

Let's not pretend to be shocked when we see facts

and attitudes that are part of everyone's repertoire when the circumstances are propitious. The big economic powers are no less selfish than we are. We must get our own house in order, fill in the cracks, and reinforce the foundation before proceeding with our customary complaints. Our hunger, our illiteracy, our unemployment, our naked children, and our needy elderly are part of another of our exclusive and shameful possessions: our errors.

We can accuse the big powers of not being generous--of not being as generous as they should be. But let's accuse ourselves of not having given access to the sea to the landlocked nations. Let's accuse ourselves of not having lifted a finger to alleviate the suffering in Haiti. Let's accuse ourselves of an unhealthy nationalism and parochial fleecing. Since for the moment it's impossible for us to be rich in body, let's be rich in spirit.

Indeed we do strive for development and progress, but what are progress and development all about? The question is not Byzantine. Not at all. At this point everyone is exhausted from so much reading and steril discussion. Development is the process of becoming more and more complex, which permits man to be incorporated into the stream of progress. Progress is nothing more than discovering and utilizing new means of handling matter (or ideas) in search of a more pleasant existence on this planet. Let's get away from these definitions before it all becomes idle chatter. The real problem is that it's simply not enough to get adequate amounts of protein or be adequately clothed, or have a roof over our heads, or have schools or hospitals--goals which, by the way, have not been reached in our countries. The real problem is that progress is defined, determined, and given shape in the developed nations, and 90% of the time in the United States. To blame the Americans for this would be as unjust as condemning Edison for inventing the electric bulb or IBM for unleashing the computer age. Edison could have been a Gómez. No one can be held accountable for his accomplishments.

"Development," which is necessary, as we've already said, if we are to become beneficiaries of "progress," exists in our countries in its most rudimentary form. For us it's primarily a matter of filling bellies, preventing our infants from dying, and teaching people to read, etc.--areas where we have had less than flattering success. In other words laying the basic infrastructure of progress. Once this is accomplished, then all secondary needs will fall into place. Progress and prosperity consist of converting tertiary and secondary necessities into primary ones. The use of electricity that yesterday was a matter of witchcraft today is--or should be--everyone's patrimony. That's the fate of all self-propelled vehicles. And it will also be the destiny of the electric toothbrush or contact lenses. Marcuse--fortunately ignored nowadays--and all his followers who cry out against the dominion of the growing complexity of appliances, utensils, and electronic gadgets have embarked without doubt on the futile adventure of trying to stop the mechanism that causes humanity to progress. Words! Simply juggling words.

Now let me return to my original train of thought. With the exception of goofy chauvinists, we all recognize the subsidiary role of what we like to call "the third world." How can the dependency be broken? If tomorrow we were succussful in meeting the primary needs of our masses, we would be disappointed to learn that our relationship with the wealthy nations had not undergone significant changes. There is only one way: to try, like present-day Europe with her common market, to modify our models of progress and development. To try to take away from the United States the power to decide what is progress and to take it away from her on the legitimate grounds of technology. All this seems to be a lunatic's delirium, but I don't see any other means of escaping from cultural backwardness. The logic is obvious: as long as the norms of civilization are dictated to us from outside, we will never be satisfied with our role. Gandhi, who thought long and hard about all these matters, finally proposed a ridiculous and desperate solution: cancel all plans for the industrialization of India and return to the never-changing Middle Ages. To ignore, because they were unattainable, the wealthy western models. No example of voluntary retrogression can be found in history. It exists only as a form of literary entertainment. Zero growth proposed and later rejected by the sages of Rome is as absurd as Gandhi's recommendation.

But if we are presently struggling for mere subsistence, how can we talk of taking over the leadership of civilization? How should I know? There _are_ formulas for putting prostrate nations on their feet. Good examples are Japan and Germany. It's not a task of years but of decades. An undertaking of extremely long duration. But even if the task were unattainable and the project farfetched, the problem which afflicts us now would still be in force. We would follow forever the carrot dangling before our eyes. Either we stew in the rancor of our own dissatisfaction or we make a commitment to work miracles. But those miracles must be performed within certain correlated ethics. Development cannot be an alibi for dictators, among other things, because there is not any reliable evidence that proves that dictatorships are more efficient at creating wealth.

THE THEME OF OUR TIME

Can the economic structure of a country be modified substantially without implanting a dictatorship? Can a nation's income be redistributed in an equitable manner without establishing an authoritarian regime? Concretely, can an authentic revolution be successfully carried out without eliminating human rights? This is the crux of the matter reduced to its most elementary form. Nevertheless, it happens that the mere formulation of the question constitutes a malevolent skirting of the real problem. This error of method, shall we say, or illogical focus is capable of pushing many countries to the brink of civil war. Perhaps in order to change a country's economic structure it is indispensable to modify its thought process by decreeing rigor, hierarchy, and an order of priorities for our own theoretical scaffolding.

We who are in favor of change want a just society. That is the basic objective. In other words, at the top of our list of values we put Justice. Now we must ask ourselves if we understand Justice to be an abolute value that encompasses all the facets of human relationships or if it is restricted to the equitable distribution of wealth. I fear that for many revolutionaries Justice is eating the same food, dressing alike, and having equal opportunities. This means that their perception of a just deed is obtained only through the distribution of physical wealth. This rudimentary interpretation of the value of justice invalidates, for example, the tremendous injustice that exists when only one privileged sector of society is the one that dictates the rules of the game. Behind the books of rationing stamps that assure equal amounts of food for each individual, an obvious symbol of a just society, is hidden violent aggressions against the rights of the individual and society as a whole. Justice is bread, but not bread alone.

Everything that we've said stems from reflections on economic inventory. Two pillars support progressive ideology; one takes stock of existing assets and then orders the redistribution of them, and the second one tries to create wealth by developing natural resources. To subscribe to these two objectives is to become a member of the "revolutionary" group. If a previous analysis of what Justice means for each of us is necessary (and we realize that the egalitarian possession of wealth is just one aspect of the problem) to distribute wealth "justly" in order to judge the revolution in abstract, one must start by analyzing the phenomenon of development. Here total confusion reigns between means and ends, between tools and objectives. "Nationalization," for example, is generally accepted as a revolutionary measure, without considering that it will be considered revolutionary only if it accomplishes its goals of development and progress.

To change the system of ownership from private hands to the state is strictly a legal matter. To congratulate the hungry peasant because he has kicked out the old boss, without tempering his hunger, without giving his children an education, without finding a decent market for his produce, is an act of the most base demagoguery. To speak of "revolution" when a foreign company is expelled and its property confiscated without a change which brings about an authentic and permanent improvement for the nation is to insult the intelligence of its citizenry. To apply the simplistic formulas of the extremists' little books without foreseeing the results, without a previous and realistic survey of the economic possibilities of the country, without a serious analysis of the circumstances that are present in each case, is not "having a revolution" but making a painful and ridiculous mistake. Latifundios are done away with, foreign companies are confiscated, not because doing so has any significance *per se*, but because the change will bring about specific benefits for the development of the nation.

Things being this way, the ill-stated question posed at the beginning of this discussion begins to make sense. If modification of the economic structure is attempted from an erroneous perspective, and it brings consequential economic chaos, there will be no other solution than to support the government with bayonets. If the ballot box is still in use, the nation will reject those who were responsible for the disaster. No one will voluntarily accept the monstrosity of sacrificing three generations for the shaky promise of a glowing future. If the "redistribution-of-the-national-income-at-an-equal-level" consists of impoverishing the former privileged class without a proportional rise in the standard of living of those who were already poor, naturally in the elections the people will hold the authorities responsible for their mistake, and only the government that resorts to the use of force will be able to stay in power.

So in order to delineate with honesty and justice the theme of our Hispanic-American era we must begin to qualify it. Can a revolution that tears down economic structures without foreseeing the results and fails to provide any kind of transitional adjustment be accomplished by democratic means? Obviously not. It would have to be kept in power by brute force. Can one play frivolously at the game of revolution, further ruin poor and underdeveloped countries, exhaust economic reserves on wild plans, and aspire at the same time to have the approval of the majority? Obviously not. Only terror will keep the authors of the disaster in power.

Now things are becoming clearer. In reality the theme of our time is not stated honestly. It is used as the first alibi on the road that leads to tyranny. The question, naively distorted, is the bayonet's disguise. A cheap excuse that usually results in violence and inefficiency. The next step in the failure will be the lies and the transferring of the responsibility of the disaster to other latitudes. The quest for a convenient scapegoat which usually happens at the meetings of UNCTAD.

ABOUT HUNGER, PEOPLE AND FOOLISHNESS

The World Conference on Population met painfully in Bucharest. As things usually go nowadays, serious and scientific discussion broke up in disorder. The "Third World" began to shout out against the "first world." The danger, they said, is no longer the unbridled population explosion mainly in the southern hemisphere but the exaggerated consumerism of those who live in the northern hemisphere. The developed countries, imperialism, colonialism, and neocolonialism are responsible for the approaching crisis. Obviously, little came out of the meeting. They should have approached the meeting with a certain degree of objectivity, but instead they came with fiery speeches and wild accusations.

Basically they are different problems. It's true that the developed nations consume inordinately, and also it's true that the demographic growth of many countries in the third world annihilates possibilities for development. One doesn't exclude the other. Or to put it another way--greed doesn't excuse irresponsibility.

But there is one basic lie which should be refuted: the curious idea that the wealthy nations have obtained their wealth at the expense of the poor ones. What abusive imperialism did Sweden use to obtain her wealth? How many Swiss, Norwegian, Danish, Australian, Czech, or Finnish expeditions have been sent out to sack the nations of our shining Third World? And Japan and Germany? Since 1945--zero hour for these countries--how many nations have they trampled? Isn't it Spain, Portugal, and Turkey--precisely the most tenacious empires--that still have one foot in underdevelopment? It is not fair to reduce the origin of these economic differences to this Manichean formula. In India there is hunger because there has always been hunger, centuries before the English arrived, and because to eradicate it is a task of massive education, of technological evolution, and of changing values that have been in force for millennia. Latin America is in the same boat. The majority of our misfortunes are of our own doing. It is true that in the 19th and 20th centuries the United States cruelly mutilated Mexico, became master of the Caribbean and Central America, and dictated one-sided norms for commerce. But that does not explain the hunger in the Andean Plateau, the Uruguayan bankruptcy, or the frightening economic structure of Haiti. It was we, bogged down in the structure and values of the colonial period, with half-built republics, who failed to carry out the necessary reforms. To our shame, even today, in the midst of a torrent of patriotic words the imperialitic enterprise pays more and better than the one owned by the indigenous oligarchy.

But all this discussion started with overpopulation. In Bucharest they said that plans to control it were sinister plots of the developed countries to keep their empires alive. And people have talked proudly about the role of the large family concerning the building of a bright future. The example of the swarming Chinese with thousands of men carrying sand on their backs to build a dam seems to dazzle the demagogues. Haven't these gentlemen ever seen a peasant threatened by the mouths of ten hungry children? Don't they realize the horror of building a dam by human traction? Perhaps China with her 800 million souls had no other alternative but to organize herself in hives, but why copy a system that is nothing more than a result of conflict between economy and demography? The peasant or worker that can't support a large family is not an abstract political or economic problem but a desperate man of flesh and blood with his helpless offspring. An irresponsible birthrate is a very serious matter to be used for demagoguery or for talking nonsense. In Rome, Proletarius was the provider of proles (progeny) for the most despicable work. Later Marx changed its meaning. Do these revolutionaries want to go back to Roman times?

But even more incomprehensible than this unreasonable position is the Vatican's attitude. The Vatican uses ethical reasons for its arguments. Rome opposes any birth control that is not done by natural means. Only abstinence and the Ogino method--Vatican roulette as it is called by some irreverent folks--are authorized as sinless. And the confusing thing for the Catholic flock is that the liberal parish priest authorizes what Rome forbids. Sooner or later the Church will cede. It's impossible for a religion as generous, open, and universal as Christianity to be obstinate concerning the irrelevant vigilance of hormonal secretions. Forcing the faithful to submit to the rhythm method which is martial and neurotic is possibly unhealthy, and it's absolutely inhuman to demand abstinence. In spite of good intentions, it's naive to maintain that reproduction is the sole purpose of copulation. The great moral revolution of our time is that sex is no longer considered an ethical matter but strictly a biological one. Today it is the couple that should responsibly decide. In the final analysis it is the prerogative of the woman to decide whether she is to become the recipient of another life. Regarding governments, they should either encourage, stabilize, or reduce the birth rate according to their own particular demographic characteristics. But all this should be in the hands of scientists and not haranguers. If it's not, we will become bogged down in the rhetoric of the Third World. The first serious scientific step may be to discuss the very existence of this "Third World" that we so often mention.

THE MYTH OF THE THIRD WORLD

Let's talk about "myths." About lies that have been consecrated by popular belief. About ghosts that sit at our tables, appear in our books and on our TV screens and finally end up penetrating our brains. A little reflection will prove to us that we have been duped for quite some time. Ghosts don't exist.

The "Third World"; the term really caught on. It has become a part of everyone's political-economic vocabulary. Two dinky little words, Indian file, that encompass the social realities of Mexico, Andalusia, and the Republic of Chad. A concept that puts Brazil and Tanzania in the same column. It makes no difference whatsoever that the economic, ethnic, juridical, and historical composition, etc. of Mexico and Chad have no remote similarities; but thanks to the revolutionary scholasticism presently in force, both countries belong to the "Third World." The rationale for establishing the relationship begins with the observation that both countries differ substantially from either the United States or England. This rationale--utter foolishness-is something like putting eggs and chairs together because they are different from elephants. If a concept is really to make a contribution to the exchange of ideas, it cannot be a mere simplification of very complex realities.

"Third World" means absolutely nothing. To attempt to organize a solid link between non-industrialized nations for purposes of opposing industrialized ones is first, an absurdity; second, a childish idea of cafe-revolutionaries; and third, suicide. Sounding the patriotic trumpet to the impoverished masses of the "Third World" is no more than a stanza composed in poor taste within the limits of today's worst ideological lyricism. There are impoverished masses, there are exploiters, there are economic interests that care more about their bank accounts than the people. But there is a big gap between recognizing those plain and painful facts and enlisting in a group that doesn't exist in order to solve them. An incredibly big gap. Each country or each region with similar problems and solutions must try to find the means of facing their own particular reality. In the sixties some absurd conventions of "Tri-Continental" delegates were organized in Havana. That comic orchestra which was multiracial, polyglot, and heterogeneous to the point of hysteria didn't work well under the direction of the Cuban Prince's baton. It's difficult to successfully direct throngs of eggs and chairs who are fighting against elephants.

The new contender for the leadership of the Third World is China. The Chinese are dazzled by the possibilities of being the leader of the poor nations (the rich nations have never even entertained the idea) and of inserting a ragged wedge between its Russian and North American rivals (in that order). Actually China's aspiration is less unrealistic than Cuba's. To begin with, the Chinese possess a few status symbols: atomic weapons, a heroic and solitary satellite, a powerful army, territory and population. The rest--"industrialization," a market composed of a hundred million people, "a healthy economy"--is created by popular imagination and ignorance in equal doses. Many decades will have to pass before China becomes an economic power. In the meantime--a long meantime--she will have to be satisfied with manipulating public opinion by waving her symbols; for example, nuclear explosions, launching artificial satellites, and military parades. But in spite of having these elements, China is forgetting the most important thing: the "Third World" doesn't exist. It's an entelechy, a mere verbal construction. It's a trick done by magicians of today's most elemental political "amateurism." An idiotic way of facing our responsibilities by using the simple procedure of simplifying the enormous complexity of the different levels of economic development in a poor "world"--the one we belong to--which is sacked by the inclement world of the rich. The rich steal everything from us: raw materials, labor, even brains. The "case" of the brain drain deserves special consideration. Let's examine it.

THEY ARE ROBBING US OF OUR BRAINS

It seems that our brains, like Papillon, flee our Hispanic environment. Bad news. It takes too much effort and money to train a biped from the thumb sucking stage to the time when he can build bridges and disembowel sick people to have him transfer his skills to the United States. Our brains, whenever they can, always emigrate to the United States. And, of course, that powerful country is not to blame. Unfortunately, we are. That country, like all others, although to a lesser degree, needs doctors, engineers, nurses, skilled workers. To put it simply, it offers opportunities to certain immigrants. The Hispanic world, on the other hand, closes its doors to these opportunities. The rural areas of Central America are lacking almost completely in medical attention. But all these Caribbean countries let three thousand Cuban doctors slip right through their fingers, and they ended up living in Florida. In time, and with generous means of attracting them, a good number of those gentlemen would have stayed in Latin America. The terrible human bleeding of Cuba which was caused by the exodus of half a million skilled people would have at least alleviated the needs of other underdeveloped countries. The taxes paid each year by this lively and deluded community in Florida is three times greater than the original cost of the orientation program for exiles. Something similar has been happening with Chilean exiles and immigrants. Those who fled from Allende and those who escaped from the junta have not been settling in Latin America. Each one of these men is a copious investment of thousands of dollars in knowledge and experience inevitably poured into the United States. Why did we fail to attract them? Because of the stupid requirements of our unions and professional associations? Do our countries have an intelligent immigration policy? I suspect it doesn't go beyond a tourist visa and bureaucratic restrictions. Unemployment is an alibi and not a serious argument. We have peasants and unskilled workers to spare, but we need professionals and specialists in almost all sectors of the economy. Parochialism is still strangling us.

But it's almost a cruel joke to talk about "brains" when referring to doctors, petty lawyers, engineers, and other ordinary run-of-the-mill professionals. The situation really becomes dramatic, frightening, and hair-raising when it comes to authentic brains. Imagine--and you'll have to be almost a Kafka to do so--a potential atomic genius being born in Nicaragua. Would he honestly be able to play dumb in Managua? Further imagine--for this you'd have to be a colossus of fiction--Max Planck or Einstein being born in Cuba. They probably would have played the drums splendidly, but there would have been nothing of quantum and relativity. Max Planck, as a matter of fact, tried to obtain a chair in a Spanish institution, and they refused to give it to him. Brains are born, but they are also made. They thrive within certain cultures and ours, weighted down by the secular Hispanic stupefaction concerning talent and inventiveness, is not the best medium for their growth. Let's be clear about this: it's not a question of race, a meaningless term, but cultural values, which are everything. The Sephardic Jews that emigrated to Morocco or to Salonika didn't amount to anything with their dinky shops. The Sephardic Jew who emigrated to Europe was Espinoza. The Spanish Nobel Prize winner, Severo Ochoa, had to make a beeline to the United States to unravel the secrets of DNA. If he had stayed in Spain, his brain never would have made its debut. When old and wise he returned to his country for the purpose of creating an institute for molecular research; he ended up trapped in a web of petty interests that obstructed his work. At our latitudes, of course, brains are born. And they rot. So before they rot, it's better for them to emigrate and bear fruit where they are permitted to do so. Let them go to New York where the cultural environment contains stimuli and not obstacles.

Some forty years ago, after the bloodbath of the Spanish Civil War, thousands of Spaniards, magnificently gifted and educated, knocked at America's door. Only Mexico and Argentina knew how to receive them with open arms. Only Mexico and Argentina knew how to benefit from this wave of talent and creativity. Hundreds of them-- Jiménez de Asua, Besteiro, Pitaluga and Eugenio Imaz, to mention a few--went to Cuba where most doors were closed to them. Today's Cuban exiles found themselves in a similar situation when most of America except the United States, Puerto Rico and Venezuela and all of Europe except Spain closed their doors to them. And the same thing is happening to the Chileans. It's the same old story of provincial idiocy.

Don't the Caribbean countries know that tens of thousands of able Argentineans and Uruguayans can be recruited in their countries? Don't the Bolivians know that the teachers they need are in Chile? For God's sake let's bring to an end this same old tune and stop the exodus of brains from our countries.

Let's not continue with the same old song at least until we have an honest and intelligent immigration policy, until we respect civilized cultural values in our own countries. Until this happens, it will be perfectly legitimate for our citizens to put on their backpacks and head for better destinations. But in the near future perhaps we will witness a more painful spectacle than the exodus of brains from Spain and Latin America. The breech that is opening up between our universities and the American ones is of such magnitude that probably our brains will have to emigrate completely unprepared. They will have to emigrate deprived of the last (and the next to the last) technical and cultural sacraments. Specializations which must be acquired outside our countries are beginning to become more numerous nowadays. And the amount of knowledge to which we have no access is becoming greater. Our universities have failed.

UNIVERSITIES FOR WHAT?

In Spain and Latin America almost everything has failed, but nothing has failed as miserably and systematically as higher education. It is horrifying to have to make an account of our intellectual contributions to the world. The debit is absolute. The credits rachitic. In the humanities and sciences there isn't, nor has there ever been, any Argentinean, Spanish or Uruguayan school of thought that has become renowned. Much less a Nicaraguan or Cuban one. For centuries, particularly for the last two centuries, we have descended to the role of the most miserable parasitic servitude. We think with Germany's head, with France's, with America's and of late with Russia's. It's not a matter of sickly regionalisms, but of imposing on ourselves more rigor, more seriousness; it's a matter of being more demanding of ourselves. Anyone can translate.

Our intellectual backwardness is due to a great extent to the failure of our universities. We erred when we established the objectives for these centers of learning. It was as important to engage in research and open a window to the intelligentsia of the country as to graduate professionals. The future would belong to the innovators because in the quality and quantity of the changes introduced resided the dialectic motor of progress. The Spanish-American could ill innovate if his intellectual environment was uniquely and exclusively a tardy sounding box for the more developed nations' scientific events. The university structure failed when it became stagnant with tenured chairs occupied by charlatans who learned and taught by rote. It's impossible to measure the amount of harm caused us by naive devotion to rhetoric. We suffer from an embarrassing attraction for empty words. The amount of prestige accorded our "silver tongues" is unfortunate. Speeches are still praised by the term "castelarianos[2]." The "idiot-on-the-platform" still enjoys recognition. The tormenting brand of orator that combines superfluity of context with twisted baroque metaphors and makes use of the gestures of a tenor from a comic opera and the melodramatic cadence of a Calvinist preacher. The creature who "speaks beautifully" has irreparably sterilized thousands of potentially fertile brains.

Our universities failed when they exchanged the concept of autonomy for the ivory tower and cut themselves off from the country's basic concerns (social ills, industry, labor, demography, etc.) and established lines of communication in accessory areas (politics). The university in our countries has been the catapult for politicians and one of the shortcuts to power. In spite of all the imperfections of the political parties, it is easy to find a relationship between political stability and the vitality of the parties. Be they good or bad, the struggle for power flows through them. Their sole purpose is to be the channel. The university has contributed to undermining these channels by becoming an alternative.

This dispersion--augmented by the unions, Church, and armed forces becoming politicized--explains the weakness of our political structure. The planners of our universities failed by creating hypertrophic monsters of ungovernable principles entangled in a bureaucratic web. Perhaps the universities should be divided into independent schools, centers which would not be allowed to have more than two thousand students. It's a matter of de-mythicizing the university student and his environment. This will not be an idyllic stage in which the extremists of the left or the right are licit and plausible, but a stage, and not a long one, in which one acquires some knowledge whose application, modification, or transmission will be useful or pleasant for the community. I believe that rebellion and protest are always legitimate, but they seem grotesque rites when they are practiced during only four or five years and by virtue of a temporary status that ends with graduation.

The university has failed by not coordinating its activities with the society to which it is indebted. How many university labs in Spain or Latin America do research for industry? How many of our colleges of arts and sciences have their sociologists analyzing the social mechanism, or psychologists helping those who need them most? How many medical schools have their students practicing in rural areas? How may law schools have their students protecting the rights of the destitute?

It's not true that our relative material poverty limits greater effort and bigger results. The University of Jerusalem and the Technical Institute of Haifa, both in Israel, are among the ten most important and creative university centers in the world. And the budget of those institutions does not exceed those of some of our larger universities. It's a matter of method, planning, and objectives.

Spain and Hispanic America need to come up with a logical university policy. The United States, half of Europe, and Russia have not attained excellent systems of education because of their economic strength, but, quite to the contrary, because education in those countries has made their formidable growth possible. We cannot afford to lose more time on rhetoric classes. We are running the risk of not being included in the history of contemporary culture. As it stands now, we hardly count at all.

WE DON'T THINK: THEREFORE WE DON'T EXIST

To admit it is painful, but it is imperative that we do so: we Latin Americans have never given birth to a worthwhile idea. Our contribution to Western Culture doesn't go beyond pure folklore or, at the most, art. There are no theoretical minds in our world. We think with others' heads, and we suffer with our own. As far as the creation of culture is concerned, we humbly resign ourselves to being interpreters without even trying to be composers. We get as far as Justo Sierra or Varona but never as far as Comte. We have produced a Vaz Ferreira and a Korn, but we have never had an Ortega. Our geniuses are faithful, loyal, and competent transmitters of the ideas of others.

Rather than being cultural milestones they are merely agents of culture. There is no doubt that their achievements are important. Without the "masters" Vasconcelos, Frondizi, Hostos, Bello, or Zea we would revert to the jungle, but Hispanic America, with its two hundred million inhabitants, four hundred years of universities, and a century and a half as republics should make a more serious effort than we are presently making. There exists no valid justification for our undeniable intellectual poverty. Simply and brutally we have been barren of profound thought.

The dream of a "Hispanic-American culture" is impossible in a world that is tending to become homogeneous. But refusing to speculate, losing our minds to the adventure of thinking is another matter. It is shameful that no worthwhile Hispanic-American has come forward in the area of the humanities or any of its branches--sociology, anthropology, psychology, etc. This horrendous superficiality of ours has a basis that has already been mentioned: the present state of our universities. The good universities in Spain and Latin America are no more than factories that turn out professionals. The bad ones are merely distributors of diplomas. Our Ph.D.'s in most cases don't go beyond the study of history of philosophy. In other words, they only scratch the surface.

Students mechanically accumulate thousands of facts without becoming remotely acquainted with critical analysis. After four or five years of being submerged in the grossest stupidity, they emerge content with a pompous Ph.D. diploma clenched in their hands.

There are economic reasons that to a certain extent justify our desertion of the scientific laboratory. But philosophical speculation-- "philosophizing" in the broadest and most beautiful sense of the word-- basically requires dedication, methodology, and intelligence and, above all, pure love of knowledge. We, it seems, don't love knowledge. Another condition is absolutely indispensable: self-respect. I know that any German or Frenchman would look with certain suspicion on any system of ideas developed by a Paraguayan or a Honduran, but if the idea were robust, they would have no other choice than to accept it.

At some point they would become accustomed to the

idea that the Hispanic-American intelligentsia, besides being composed of plastic artists and writers of fiction, also includes people capable of deep thought, audacious explorers of abysses. Until this happens, we will simply be what we are now: picturesque.

NOTES

[1] Latifundio. A vast tract of land belonging to a single landowner.

[2] Emilio Castelar. 19th century Spanish writer, politician, and famous orator.

IV

DIVING IN THE MELTING POT

THE BABY'S PARENTS

There is nothing more pathetic than the naiveté of an anti-American Englishman. The United States is England naked. England without her derby hats, her umbrellas, her "gentlemen," her "sirs" and "lords" and without her five o'clock tea. England without her nobility and weighty burden of tradition. It's England in its Common Law, Newton, Hobbes, Parliament, Darwin and Spencer, and in her worship of her never sufficiently praised "common sense." The United States kept the institution but discarded the tradition. It took the social mentality which is aimed at progress and always open to dialogue and tolerance, and it left behind the complex class system of a nation with a thousand years of continuous history. In America, English virtues and defects took on an incredible vigor. We must understand this if we are to avoid the mistake made by Ortega y Gasset,[1] who believed that the United States was a nation without history bordering on barbarism. What was really just beginning was society not history, which is very different. Society--no matter what kind it is--with its hierarchies, its powerful, and its untouchables is always unjust. The closer we are to its origins, the more possible it is for talent to come forward and manifest itself.

A similar phenomenon occurred in Latin America in the 1930's with respect to Spain. Argentina greatly surpassed the Spanish model in the areas of economic development and distribution of wealth. Then Peronism and other calamities led the country astray, but it was obvious that the offspring was more vigorous than the mother country. Later on we will come back to this particular point. Right now just let me point out one of the norms of colonial development. Provided that fiscal conditions allow it, colonies once established surpass the original model. Brazil compared with Portugal and the United States, Canada, and Australia compared with England are good examples. And probably this phenomenon is due to the freedom of movement that exists in a society free from a frozen class structure. Perhaps the American worship of individual initiative and the self-made man have a common origin: the historical rejection of a parasitic nobility that did not confirm and sustain its merits. These factors endorse the sacredness of the common citizen, equality, and the absence of protocol.

And What About the Non-English?

There are no non-English. The United States has integrated great masses of Poles, Africans, Irish, Indians, Russian Jews, Scandinavians, Mexicans-- in essence, fauna of every kind--but the mixture ended up being essentially Britannic. In the United States anything that is not British is folklore. Like jazz and soul. Pure tourist attractions. Americans themselves travel to St. Augustine in Florida or to New Orleans in Louisiana to be tourists in these other countries of suspicious meridional background. Moreover, the citizenry of British origin controls for the most part finances, politics, and industry. Some maintain that the Jews control the finances, but this is abysmally inexact. The Jews, in fact, do enjoy a more significant economic importance than their number might suggest, but they are far from "controlling finances." The Russian Jews, nevertheless, were the ethnic minority that were best and most rapidly integrated into society. They are closely followed by the Swedes.

In any case, the success of the United States as a nation consists of having fused all European nationalities and no small number of Asians, Africans, and Latin Americans into what's known as "the American." In judging America's cultural and scientific contribution there is no argument more unjust or degrading than the one that attributes her successes to European talent bought by the Americans. That talent didn't flourish because it was European, but because it found fertile ground in the United States. Any race or people that live in an adequate cultural environment will produce the same results. To think otherwise is gross racism.

The Anglo-American absorption of the different ethnic groups--blacks, Indians, Mexicans, Cuban mulattoes, Puerto Ricans--hasn't been and isn't easy. Unfortunately an absence of racial prejudice is not one of the English virtues. If these ethnic minorities eventually find their place in the sun in that society, it's essentially because of that country's respect for the law. That same law that called out the army to open the door to a university for the black student Meredith, or that law that takes control of a city to force integration in public schools. Perhaps the essential difference between Anglo-Saxon and Hispanic racism, and of course here I include Latin America also, lies in the limited relationship between our social behavior and our laws. Our laws sanction the most absolute equality, while our society practices racism to one degree or another largely without even being perceived. The white Andean oligarchy's disdain for the Indian or the "cholo,"[2] the white Cuban's contempt for colored Cubans, or the Spaniard's scorn of the Gypsy or the "Moor" are facts that are easily documented. But because our legislation doesn't reflect this racism, we are incapable of generating measures to alter the situation. In Spain, for example, Gypsies are practically non-existent in the power structure, and in Cuba only 7% of the members of the Central Committee of the Communist Party are black. In Latin America we completely ignore our racism.

Americans, conscious of their racism, have, on the other hand, very concrete goals. If blacks constitute 15% of the population, they should benefit from the national income and participate in the leadership to the same extent. The rationale is as cold as it is just. Today they are far from accomplishing this goal, but if any white nation has the possibility of really integrating the black minority, it's the United States. As things stand now, the least African of all blacks on the planet are the American blacks. While in Brazil, Haiti, Cuba, Panama, and the Dominican Republic the blacks maintain their habits, customs, religion, and at times even African languages, the blacks in the United States are culturally Europeans--Anglo-Saxon protestants--in spite of jazz, soul, and some other "typical" characteristics. When the "Black Panthers" dabbled with a return to Africanism, they found out that the American cultural environment was much more binding than the color of their skin.

Nationalism?

The amalgam of peoples and races a la Britannia regulated by respect for law and order has ended up eliminating nationalism. The American has opted for having purely aseptic and rational ties with his country. Nationalism is always an emotional phenomenon. An affiliation that at one extreme is love for a country and at the other extreme hate for any other kind of affiliation. Nationalism ends up being the acceptance of one of the most cruel stupidities ever uttered: "My country right or wrong." Today's _Gringos_ --millions of them--look at the United States in another light. Not as a mystical mother that demands sacrifice--the ever-bloody "motherland"--but as a place which provides work, study, pleasure, and in which they fortuitously and arbitrarily happen to live. Jingoism is a thing of the past. Here we have the healthiest proof of British common sense. If the Vietnam war is an absurdity, a crime, or a useless massacre, American flags are burned as a sign of protest. If your country is not right, you are against it. It's as simple as that. Nationalism is disappearing from the repertoire of attitudes. Patriotism, which to a certain extent is the liturgy of nationalism, has even less of a future. Patriotism is also disappearing.

The End of Patriotism

The American revolution is profound and drastic. From where I stand, Brezhnev and Mao now seem like two soft, timid, drowsy _petits bourgeois_. One of the most significant aspects of the American Revolution which exploded in the decade of the 60's is the disappearance of the civic virtue patriotism. They've said to hell with the national anthem, the flag, national heroes, and all varieties of patriotic rhetoric. The lunar generation has thrown out these traditions as if they were an unwelcome guest. Jefferson with his proverbial wisdom, Washington who couldn't lie about the cherry tree, and old Honest Abe have all lost their mythical halos that conferred on them their heroic status. Nowadays they are the subject of brazen jokes, obscene graffiti, and irreverent drawings that haven't abated even with the bicentennial.

American humor, which is much "blacker" than Britain's, has been the battering ram responsible for this destruction. The beautiful myths have come tumbling down. Few people became upset when hundreds of university students carried Viet Cong flags and cried out for the enemy's victory. Actually their enemy is simply someone indicated by their conscience at a given moment. _A priori_ loyalty has disappeared from the political arena.

To be honest, these extreme examples of "apatriotism"--this new word has become absolutely indispensable--can be found only among a very small minority. But it's merely a question of degrees; non-extremists don't get excited about patriotic things either. Besides, the phenomenon is irreversible. There will be no resurgence of a patriotic spirit unless the nation finds itself in danger of becoming involved in a world war. Patriotism, like any other aspect of culure, survives only if it's transmitted from one generation to the next and if it's fed periodically with new myths and if secular fetishes are revitalized. When the lunar generation comes to power and begins to rule, order, and transmit, even more of the old rhetoric will be left out.

From all indications, it seems apparent that this phenomenon is indeed taking place; therefore, it becomes inevitable to inquire fearfully whether it's possible for a nation to survive without patriots. Are patriotic myths indispensable for the preservation of a nation? Or can other myths take their place? Throughout history patriotism, religion, and language have been the factors that have provided the greatest degree of cohesion. The first two are presently dying in the United States.

However, not everything calls for alarm. To counterbalance this phenomenon, another myth is being erected. Another formidable cohesive factor is appearing: the mastery of technology. This prodigious manipulation of matter is making the United States a country different from all the rest. The mastery of science fosters the deterioration of metaphysical myths, but it has created another myth: the scientific one. Science is shaping the United States in such a peculiar fashion that it will end up being radically different from the rest of the world. This will tend to make the country more homogenous. Here, within this fetish, lies its present centripetal force. Perhaps this new myth will allow it to cast aside old bonds.

While the Soviet Union, conservative and reactionary, becomes entrenched in her irrational nationalism a la Ivan the Terrible, in the United States we are witnessing an authentic revolution which is both risky and harrowing. A nation that is colonizing the world without having to count on its patriots. A country that is testing the possibility of existing without patriotism.

Now then, let's accept that the imprint on that civilization is English. Let's admit that its citizenry is increasingly becoming fused in a mass far removed from nationalistic rhetoric; nevertheless, certain minorities will always remain outside of this picture. Some minorities like the pre-Columbian Indians that have been crushed but have not disappeared.

ABOUT THE SIOUX AND OTHER MARGINAL GROUPS

Redskins and palefaces scalped each other once again. The story up to this point is just a picturesque anecdote; however, from here on out--and this is the sad part--we run into a whole slew of absurdities. Let's get straight to the point by drawing a conclusion that is as grotesque as it is inexorable: throughout history crimes have been condoned. Injustice and abuse triumph and become immutable realities on which we have to base a new system of evaluation. It's true that the whites drove them from their lands, and it's true that they committed thousands of outrages; but it's also true that those 351 treaties violated by the Anglo-Saxons are valuable only as museum pieces. Today can we justify giving back land to the Sioux? Just as well as we could justify returning Guatemala to the Mayas, Chile to the Araucanians or Peru to the Incas. Is it true that the Yankees committed innumerable crimes against the indigenous population? Of course they did! They are as infamous as anyone else who undertakes an expansionistic campaign. Or are the crimes committed by the Hispanic Creoles less horrendous than those of Custer's gang? Sarmiento, Avellaneda and Mitre decimated the Argentinean Indians approximately during the same period that the U.S. Cavalry was doing its thing. In the Argentinean battalions along with the bugler and the sergeant, there was an official executioner whose sole function was to slit Indians' throats. During the Conquest, the Spaniards practically annihilated all the Indians in the Antilles. In addition to that, in 1912 white Cuban Creoles killed close to one thousand blacks in a shameless racial war.

Concerning the incident at Wounded Knee, there was an article in the Spanish press comparing the Anglo-Saxon conquest and colonization with their

Spanish counterparts, and the conclusion regarding the treatment of the natives was that Spain had been more merciful. What remarkable naiveté. The Spanish crown could not have been more merciful with the Indians than it was with the Spaniards themselves. If the rebellions in the peninsula had been stifled by bloodshed, why would the means of dealing with the remote "savage" be different? If Aztecs, Incas or Mayans weren't exterminated, it was because they already had organized nuclei of great density and their social structure was suitable for acculturation and consequently was a source of manual labor. When the Spaniards encountered Indians with characteristics similar to those in the United States--warlike, nomadic, indomitable--they reacted with the same severity. For example, the Araucanians, the Caribs and the Patagonian Indians. Father Las Casas exaggerated, but he didn't make things up.

In essence what I'm trying to say is that neither Spain nor the United States nor Hispanic America can justify their past atrocities by pointing to those of the other country. Neither do these atrocities serve as a point of departure for analyzing the plight of the various marginal groups. The problem is much more serious, and I'm afraid there is no ideal solution. What should Mexico, Chile or the United States do with the pre-Columbian cultures that have survived? Should these countries encourage their marginality by helping them preserve their own culture? Should they respect the integrity of these races? Or should they try to incorporate them into European patterns? Are reservations morally right? Is it right to raise generations of Sioux or Araucanians in test tubes? Because reservations are test tubes, circus tents or anything but a healthy and well-balanced environment. A family, wearing feathers and claiming to be Lutherans, sitting inside a canvas tent watching TV is a bad joke. On the other hand, it's a flagrant abuse to force these marginal groups to integrate into a society that is not theirs or make them unhappy by having to live in Boston, Valparaiso or Mexico City. Railing at Sarmiento or Buffalo Bill is pointless. The problem exists here and now and affects <u>several million</u> human beings. The solution must be sought by <u>both</u> the marginal groups and those responsible for keeping them in their marginal state. Either you commit the injustice of perpetuating the infamous alienation of the reservation or you commit injustice by integrating the marginal groups into the culture of the established society. There is no ideal solution.

Either way, the marginal groups will suffer. If I had to choose between the insanity of the reservations and the violence of acculturation, I think I would opt for the second choice because even if it is more painful, in the long run it will eventually solve the problem. This means, and I make no bones about it, that it would be better for the Sioux, the Araucanians, the Puerto Ricans in New York, the Cubans in Miami and any other marginal groups that exist in this imperfect world to become part of their own immediate national environment and abandon those alienating worlds in which they live. César Chávez and his Mexican-Americans are mistaken; the road they have chosen tends to perpetuate their painful marginality.

A few years ago this position would have been branded as imperialistic or God knows what. I don't think it's a panacea. It just seems to me to be the lesser of several evils. Europe has been a vertiginous unifier. The whole globe bears her stamp. This has been both advantageous and unjust. On the road to unification languages and dress, religious and artistic forms have been brutally wiped out. Civilizations have disappeared, and vestiges of ancient peoples have been eradicated. The pre-Columbian Indians are on the list of the defeated. What's done is done. I know that asking for the incorporation of marginal groups is almost like asking for the conclusion of an uncompleted crime, but it would be worse to leave a few of them in perpetual agony. Of course I'm not talking about forced acculturation, but about providing economic resources that would make acculturation possible. I'm talking about abolishing the cultural ghetto by providing economic opportunities, education, etc. Aiding these marginal groups to prevent the suffering of future generations. It's a terrible solution, but at least it's a solution. The black problem is different. In fact, the white racists are the ones with the problem. Unlike the Indians, the American black's culture is not isolated and stagnant. Culturally they are Anglo-Saxon and as I've already said, more Europeanized than any other blacks in the Americas. This factor provides the black race with channels that lead to an egalitarian society. It's quite obvious that this kind of integration can't be accomplished by decree. It's a profound and difficult social problem, but it appears that the United States is beginning to make some headway.

Deep down inside, the majority of whites seem to be substantially altering certain behavioral patterns.

THE WHITE REVOLUTION IN THE USA

Because of some atrocity committed by white racists in Arkansas, Nicolás Guillén wrote a bitter poem in which he spoke of black children who "went to school among pedagogical rifles." Since that time--in just a few years--the panorama has changed. The United States is accomplishing racial integration at a rate unprecedented in modern history. The Yankees' racial revolution doesn't depend on the attitude of the black extremists as is supposed by some simpletons. These extremists are more like counter-revolutionaries. The trumpet blast of the blacks-- *piano* in Martin Luther King, *fortissimo* in Cleaver--has created among whites an awareness of an embarrassing, unjust, and degrading situation.

Obviously the revolution couldn't be accomplished by 11% of the population--the blacks who, in addition account for the weakest sectors of the American economic structure. The revolution had to come from that other 89% of the population--the whites, accustomed to privilege and prejudice.

First they did away with the most blatant signs of discrimination; they discontinued separate areas in public transportation, separate water fountains and different restrooms, etc. But none of this is really important. In the whole nation's psyche--and this is the extraordinary part--a change began taking place which enabled them to appreciate the blacks' predicament.

The aesthetic canons took a new turn. Broad noses, kinky hair and dark skin magically became beautiful. White women allowed black men to embrace them--and vice versa--in a healthy and increasing degree of inter-racial contacts. (What other means is there to confer homogeneity on a nation--which is indispensable for her survival as a univocal entity--if it's not miscegenation?)

Doors were opened to the talents of hundreds of black professors, scientists, and writers whereas before only folkloric or athletic contributions were acceptable. They went even further. They adopted, as a compensatory measure--if such a thing is possible--reverse discrimination which favors blacks. Today big universities are open to racial minorities in spite of the fact that their academic averages are often inferior to those of whites that have been rejected. Public schools were forced to integrate black and white students knowing full well that the scholastic level of those integrated schools would drop. More and more frequently the political parties are nominating black candidates and the public is electing them to key positions. There was some talk about Stokes, Cleveland's mayor, or Brooke, the influential senator from Massachusetts--both black, being nominated as candidate for the vice-presidency of the United States. Something like this is bound to happen in the near future.

This fulminating ascent of the black has had a tremendous psychological impact on the country's black youth. Having left behind a position of inferiority and frustration, some have assumed an attitude of aggression and insolence. It's only natural for this to happen. Maybe it's even healthy. The fist lifted high fortunately won't overthrow the government or crush its institutions, but it will at least free the young black from the nightmares of his shackled grandparents, from his submissive parents, from his age-old fear of the white man and from his unsatisfied desire for the inaccessible white woman. If his present anger acts as a purging agent which helps him build a new image of himself, then it's welcome indeed. For the future mestizo nation it would be better if his head were held high.

If there is something that characterizes American society it is that secret centripetal force that has obliterated the countries of origin of millions of emigrants. Legions of Italians, Irish, Jews from every imaginable place, Japanese and Mexicans have landed on America's muscular belly. For centuries that incredible homogenizing force has been at work absorbing Americans of African ancestry. It's not a matter of simply changing a few things for the sake of appearances. It's a genuine racial revolution that has been accomplished in a minimum amount of time.

Paradoxically the reactionary groups that are hindering racial integration are black as well as white. On the one hand there are the southern racists; on the other the "Black Panthers", the "Black Muslims," and all the black rivals of the KKK who dream of creating black republics and other racial monsters of this sort. However, both white and black extremists will be suddenly defeated; the racial revolution has begun, and it's useless trying to stall it. Fortunately, helping to reinforce it is an appreciable increase in the number of interracial marriages.

Sexual Revolution vs. Black Revolution

Fortunately for the United States, two simultaneous revolutions are presently in progress, the revolution of the black masses and the sexual revolution. Twenty million blacks are demanding better conditions within that robust "American way of life" at the same time that a belligerent generation is shedding the last vestiges of the austere society molded by a handful of fanatical pilgrims. Of the two revolutions, obviously the most dangerous one is the racial revolution. In the most stident sectors of the black minority the tone of the demands is almost belligerent. There is talk of urban guerrillas, "black republics" and other ideas which by virtue of being radical are explosive. In dealing with black extremists, American society has resorted to police brutality. Absolutely necessary to be sure, but nevertheless regrettable.

However, another more effective weapon has appeared without anyone noticing it: the sexual revolution. In a way the sexual revolution is the counter-black revolution. Instead of fighting the blacks face to face, more subtle methods are being used. Defeat is being inflicted by using benevolent means. They are being pacified by an old procedure. The solution is an ideal one and the only possible one: increased miscegenation. The mulattoes are the only ones who will be able to put an end to the squabble between the blacks and the whites.

At the time of the Civil War in the United States, Negroes made up 20% of the total population. Today they comprise only 11%. The decrease is due to the fabulous increase in European immigration and to the fact that blacks don't multiply faster than whites as was once believed. The barrier that prevented miscegenation was based on the supposed repugnance that blacks aroused in whites. This supposition has proven to be totally false. Moreover, centuries of strict separation of the races and a few myths divulged in whispers have awakened in the American white woman an inexplicable curiosity concerning the black male.

Sexual integration, which is the only definitive

one, is making great strides in the large cities but is progressing very slowly in small towns. The reason is obvious: the anonymity felt by the inhabitant of a large urban area frees him for the most part from social pressure. What other people say is of no consequence in New York City because, as a matter of fact, no one says anything. Nobody cares.

Paradoxically, the United States has been incredibly lucky to have had two revolutions at the same time. One of them by itself would probably have been a catastrophe.

THE HISPANICS (NOTES FOR AN IMAGINARY BESTIARY)

The Gringos have come up with a strange creature called "the Hispanic". The Hispanic is a very small dark guy with curly hair full of greasy kid stuff. The Hispanic is a fellow who is very rigid when it comes to matters of fertility and punctually gets his long-suffering Hispanic wife pregnant every nine months. The Hispanic barely gets by, living off welfare--which irritates the taxpayers--surrounded by his promiscuous, dirty, lazy, dangerous tribe. He uses knives, attacks in gangs, and not even fidgety Mr. Chakiris, rightly finished off in West Side Story, has been able to redeem him. In addition to these pretty facts, the Hispanic is lazy when he's sober, a phenomenon--I'm referring to being sober--that is rarely observed. The Hispanic habitually crosses the border as part of a large herd--provided the Ku Klux Klan or the border guards don't stop him--or he travels in dark bunches from Cuba, the Dominican Republic, or Puerto Rico. Lately there have been dense hoards of Hispanics coming from Argentina, Chile, Uruguay, Columbia and Peru. In addition, the hispanometer--a delicate instrument used by immigration officials that is sensitive to sweaty armpits and dirty feet--has noted the presence of Hispanics from Spain, the land of olés and bulls that was discovered by Admiral Ernest Hemingway during a famous trip on which red wine prevented him from finding out for whom the bells were tolling.

This Hispanic creature, cruelly characterized by Anglo-Saxon prejudice, is usually so dull that he promotes his own marginal position by emphasizing his place of origin. Because of this, the populous groups have subclassified themselves as Chicanos, Newyoricans, or Cubiches. These are the subspecies that would be noted by the Wallace-like Linnaeus on duty in Yankee customs. These Americans originally from Mexico, Cuba, or Puerto Rico don't realize that assuming the classification of Hispanic means taking on prejudices created by Yankees of northern European origin. Why aren't there "Germans" in the USA? Why don't the "Irish" account for one of the destitute minorities? Why aren't there "French" or "Slavic" groups? Hispanics exist because a discriminatory racial prejudice exists that creates the concept and probably comes from an old contempt that Northern Europe felt for her southern neighbors, especially for African Spain.

It's utter stupidity, collective suicide, to applaud the end of the Yankee melting pot only to become submerged in that bastardized melting pot in which Nordic prejudice burns the "Hispanics." What is a Hispanic? The Argentinean of Italian ancestry? The Chilean of German extraction? The Cuban whose grandparents were from Galicia and the Canary Islands? The Mexican or Peruvian Indian? The mestizo? The mulatto born in the Caribbean Islands? Perhaps it's nice to feel-proud-to- be-a "Cubiche," "Chicano" or "Newyorican," and wear, in addition, that dubious habit of "Hispanic," but that attitude only adds fuel to Anglo-Saxon racism. The struggle of American citizens coming from Latin America cannot be saved if they allow themselves to be categorized as "Hispanics" because Hispanic is not an ethnic group or a nationality. Unfortunately it's racial prejudice. Why should a white person from Buenos Aires who is an American citizen, speaks English, has blond hair and blue eyes be considered a Hispanic. On the contrary, why is a Berliner with the same characteristics just a Yankee without any other qualifications? Why is an American of Indo-Mexican ancestry a Hispanic and an American of French ancestry born in New Orleans not French? Between one and the other there are enormous prejudices. In order not to be considered Hispanic the obvious solution, even though it may be a long, slow, trying, agonizing one, is simply to stop being Hispanic. Avoid the trap of bilingualism. Frantically learn to speak English without an accent. Anglicize names and surnames. That marginal language, Spanish, will never be heard on space ships launched by NASA. The big transactions that take place in Chase Manhattan and Citibank offices will never be carried out in Spanish. It's impossible to erase prejudices, age-old prejudices, but it's possible to work around them and diffuse them. The solution is not to sanction ghettoes but to tear them down. It's not endogamy but exogamy and miscegenation. Hispanics should fight against prejudices from within American society, and not from without. By kicking and pushing they should get right in the middle of things and smother their own mythological Hispanic values. (Let Spain and Latin America be in charge of defending the ethereal values of race and spririt.) Let other imbeciles parade on "the Day of the Race"[3]--what race, for God's sake?--but not those who wish to be treated like everyone else, without prejudices. This slow process of miscegenation will probably go on for many decades, perhaps even centuries, but in the long run it will achieve beneficial results. Cultivating "Hispanity" just to have the mayor of New York City have his picture taken dressed as a Mexican cowboy on the 12th of October in my opinion is alarmingly deceitful.

A few years ago a Venezuelan journalist who was irritated by my evident admiration for certain facets of the English and American ways of life asked me why I lived in Spain and not in the United States. I answered her that I didn't care to be a Hispanic and wanted to spare myself the titanic task of becoming an (authentic) Gringo. She didn't understand what I was talking about. I hope readers of this book won't have the same problem.

At this point perhaps we should make a few comments on our own particular "melting pot" and how the peninsular Spanish coincide with and differ from the variety that took root in the Americas.

HISPANITY: GOTHS AND CREOLES

Every 12th of October we once again fall into the bad habit of celebrating the "Day of the Race." It's always the same: don Christopher, the three ships, the spiritual repository of the West, etc. In Spain during those rainy autumn days, they become afflicted with an oppressive Hispanic frenzy. During that season the laurel crowns of Ferdinand and Isabella wax green once again. Now, five centuries after the event took place, they consider it more important than when it actually occurred. For example, in the 16th century twice as many books about Turkey were published than about the new continent. East-West or Islam-Christianity, if you prefer, monopolized everyone's attention during that period. In addition, Europeans were too involved in killing each other in the Reformation and Counter-Reformation to take very seriously some dark people wearing feathers that lived way on the other side of the Atlantic. Eventually the Peninsula did spill out over the newly discovered land, and there it took root and flourished with its virtues and defects in promissory America. That--the trunk and its twenty offshoots--is what's called "Hispanity." It's strange that there's nothing that's called "Britannity" or "Gallicity." England and France have been less energetic in proclaiming their role as cultural progenitor. Probably all the to-do is the result of a set of very special circumstances. Spain's last public appearance as a world protagonist was the conquest and colonization of America. Then she hid her body from history. She didn't want anyone to see her medieval wrinkles.

During the American adventure Spain exhausted herself. She lost her initiative forever. The Renaissance brought Europe a fever that, unfortunately, Spain never contracted. That fever was a passion for progress and change. The predominant trait of Spanish society has been precisely the contrary: stubborn immutability. The Reformation, the Enlightenment, the French Revolution, the democratic-bourgeois reforms, republicanism, and lastly, liberal parliamentary Europeanism--all of these have been futile dreams of an invariably repressed segment of her population. Except for the brief glimmers of the Courts of Cadiz (1812), the trienium of 1920-1936, Spain has not known the triumph of progressive forces. This is an unusual case in the West. Probably in the world.

Based on these reflections two interesting conclusions may be drawn. First, the vast difference between the mother country and her twenty offshoots is this: fortunately Hispanic America doesn't share certain Spaniards' phobia against change. For the most part Hispanic Americans have set their sights on the innovations of modern thought. Second, neither the parent nor the offspring has had much luck at this business of progress and prosperity. Hispanic America can't use the phony excuse of being fledgling republics. There's nothing new about America. She's as old as Europe because she's nothing more than an extension of the old continent. Europe's most impressive trait has been her ability to obliterate and utterly destroy other cultures. Only vestiges remain from ancient China, India, and from pre-Columbian American. Whether it's the Soviets, or parliaments, or military dictatorships, or computers, or Coca-Cola, all the models presently in use are of European or Euro-American origin, which is one and the same, and have been adopted by the rest of the world. The color of skin, of course, is of no importance. Neither is the folkloric apparatus. What counts is the mental structure and the ideas that it nurtures. It was in this regard that Europe imprinted all the imperalistic violence imaginable, and it's not worth wasting time hurling reproaches. That's how it is, and immutably so. In spite of Fanon or Sartre. In spite of the Third World rhetoric of the new scholastics.

The difference that I pointed out between Spain and Latin America (immovability vs. progressivism) at times seems to become reversed. Today's Spaniards--except for a minuscule group of fanatics who have more bark than bite--are embarrassed about having been so impervious to progressive European thought. The nation repudiates Unamuno's[4] ludicrous comment "let *them* invent." Now, the key word is progress. On the other hand, in Latin America there are even some people who foresee some sort of downfall of civilization as a whole and the resurgence of something as little understood as the values of pre-Columbian civilization. Something similar to a new adaptation of the myth of the noble savage.

THE RESISTIBLE ASCENSION OF PRE-COLUMBIAN VALUES

Carlos Fuentes is a great Mexican novelist. First the praises so that I won't be accused of bad-mouthing anyone. I admire the author of *The Death of Artemio Cruz* and *Where the Air is Clear*. I admire less the author who wrote *The Change of Skin*, but you can't expect me to be enthralled with every line the man writes. All this came up because of a television program aired in Europe in which the famous novelist speaking on Latin American cinema postulated a certain kind of romantic nationalism and foretold the collapse of Western values--as defined by the Yankees--and as a counter-balance, the resurgence of the values of pre-Columbian civilization which has been preserved intact by the hermetic properties of the indigenous communities in Mexico and other Latin-American countries.

It seems that delusions of grandeur are inherent to our race, culture, and what have you. In the

Iberian Peninsula we had hardly gotten over the shocking news that "Spain is the repository of Western spiritual values" when we heard the blast of Fuentes' trumpet announcing that as Spain becomes exhausted, the Mayans, Zapotec and Guaraní will have their turns. Apparently we Spaniards and Latin Americans are some kind of nursery or hatchery of spiritual values. When the West is on her last leg, we'll see Spain, like in Lepanto, coming to the rescue. When even Spain succombs, the pre-Columbian civilizations will take her place. (I assume the Mohicans, lacking a quorum, will be excluded since according to all indications James Fenimore Cooper, former CIA agent, killed off the last one a century ago.)

Carlos Fuentes' naiveté is shocking. He's reacting the same way Rodó did except he writes better than the Uruguayan. There are three gross errors in his interpretation of American history. The first is to think of Latin American as an autonomous cultural entity. The second is to assume that pre-Columbian civilizations play an important factor in its creation. And the third is dividing America into "they"-- the Gringos --and "we"--the Latin Americans. If Fuentes were to realize that Latin America is a cultural extension of Europe, he would see things from a broader perspective. Southern Europe--Spain and Portugal--could not have given birth to societies totally different from their parent. They imposed the model that they had, and on top of it they superimposed the dead weight of the defeated civilizations. The end result continued being essentially European, although not necessarily white. Could you possibly find a more European spirit than Juárez? His sense of justice, his uncompromising defense of his European liberal concept of the world? Race is of little consequence. In the final analysis Turks, Armenians and Mongols have ended up becoming Europeans. Europe is not only Paris, Berlin or London. Rustic Bulgarian villages, Third World Albania, underdeveloped southern Italy, itinerant Gypsies, Greece, Spain, Portugal, with different degrees of development like Argentina are also Europe. What I'm trying to say is that the dependency and the technological and economic inferiority of certain parts of Europe in relationship to Germany and France are comparable to Latin America's relationship with the United States.

Fuentes complained about slavishly copying Yankee values and mentioned "chewing gum and Coca-Cola" being indisputable symbols of our "spiritual submission." If Fuentes recognized that his "they" and "we" dichotomy was possibly inexact, he would be more careful about what he says. _Gringos_ and Latins are part of the same European cultural heritage. Approximately a century ago the United States, Northern Europe's outpost, became the leader of that world. Before this, back in the 17th century, Iberian decline had begun, and Spain and Portugal became nations that trailed behind England, France, Holland and Germany. It's not surprising that Latin America trails along behind the United States. It's totally predictable for different sectors of a cultural system to imitate their leader's patterns. Today it's Coca-Cola, yesterday it was Britain's five o'clock tea and France's absinthe. We Latin Americans didn't even learn to smoke from the Caribbean Indians. We had to learn from the Dutch.

Concerning the resurgence of pre-Columbian values, I believe that don Carlos is out of his mind. Slowly but inexorably the vestiges of those fabulous civilizations still remaining will disappear. The trend is to become homogeneous, and the whole world is moving in the direction of European values (Europe on both sides of the Atlantic). Fuentes spoke of gum and Coca-Cola. He could just as well have said "penicillin and telephone," but the joke would have made him a victim.

Where does the denunciation and rejection of Western values come from? Probably from the frustration that is the result of comparing Latin America with the United States and verifying that we-have-lost-the-race. In another essay by Fuentes--I believe it had to do with the Latin-American narrative--there appeared very pessimistic conclusions on the growing gap between the United States and Latin America. This is true to a certain extent, but nothing is to be gained from the crazy notion of withdrawing from one's own civilization. We have to keep beating the donkey to see if he'll speed up because dismounting is insanity. It would also be a good idea to stop that Manichaean habit of using "they" and "we" as if they were two sides irreconcilably at odds wth each other. We are _all_ passengers on the same ancient and impetuous ship given birth to by Greece and educated by Rome. As on all ships, some travel first-class others third-class and from time to time some come along as stowaways.

NOTES

[1] José Ortega y Gasset (1883-1955). Spanish philosopher and essayist associated with the Generation of 1900. Some of his works are *España invertebrada*, *El tema de nuestro tiempo*, *La rebelión de las masas*, and *Mediaciones del Quijote*.

[2] Cholo. A term indicating a mestizo of white and Indian ancestry, very often pejorative.

[3] Día de la Raza. The Spanish term used for October 12, Columbus Day.

[4] Miguel de Unamuno (1864-1936). Spanish writer and philospher associated with the Generation of 1898.

V

COMPETITION, WAR, TECHNOLOGY

THE COMPETITION GAME

The fabulous Yankee energy emanates from a certain colossal superstition: competition. The Gringos think of life as a perpetual quest for personal successes and social goals. Probably all other living creatures lean in the same direction, but it's a fact that they don't feel the same compulsion to win. In that society the winner is the hero; the loser a poor devil. They talk about winner and loser instinct. Personality types guided by a hidden built-in antenna which leads to success or failure. The winner has a right to total recognition and the loser, a certain degree of contempt. The loser deserves no pity. He can't even pity himself because self-pity is an odious defect in that society. Nietzsche with his worship of superman, without having the United States in mind, set down a system of values similar to the American model. Saxon America--it has often been said--loves a winner and rejects a loser. Probably the origins of this particular mentality should be sought in the Protestant ethic and in its rigid predestination, but in these decades of interplanetary travel it makes no sense to attribute this present conduct to Lutherans, Calvinists and Quakers. It's simply a trait in the social mentality of the American, be he Catholic, Protestant, or atheist.

Does it make sense to think of life as a long series of obstacles? I don't even know if it makes sense to think of life as anything. I'm afraid that "life," that strange process of rusting out, can't be reduced to logical explanations, but I dare venture the hypothesis that, at the cultural level, competition plays a role similar to the one natural selection plays at the level of biological evolution. It doesn't escape my attention that competition in culture is rarely just since many individuals play with definite advantages, but for what it's worth, it should be pointed out that natural selection isn't just either since many fortuitous factors have consecrated or exterminated whole species. ("Justice" is simply another human invention like the toothbrush or standards of beauty.)

In any event, whether or not you disregard the preceding reflections, it is indubitable that this particular American idiosyncracy meshes well with her socio-political system and consequently yields better fruits. Political liberalism and capitalism provide a fitting framework for this great competition. The hominid with winner instincts will find ample running room; the poor guy destined to failure will find plenty, too. In short, "the system," within certain bounds and to a greater degree than the totalitarian systems, permits the individual to build his own life which is more or less autonomous and free.

Maybe the tremendous expansion of American capitalism should be explained in terms of the stampede in search of personal success. This is the controversial rat race referred to by sociologists. For this rat race there's no better track than the one provided by an open economic and political system. In that country the stories about certain individuals who go from rags to riches are indeed true. This particular kind of winner is known as the "self-made man" who within that set of values is more meritorious than the gentlemen who inherited everything because the history of every American starts with the individual himself as has already been pointed out in another part of this book.

A Value Judgment

Is the rat race legitimate? Is it right to base the whole purpose of human existence totally on personal success? You have to keep asking questions to get to the heart of the matter. Is a totalitarian society legitimate? One that arbitrarily assigns a salary, books, basic ideas, roles. Is a contemplative society where man vegetates and has no other goal than adoring God (the Trappists) or his own social marginality (the hippies) legitimate? If I had to choose, the Yankee alternative seems the most hospitable to me, not only for its worship of the winner but because of the social methods of mitigating the loser's failure. The totalitarian option contains too many personal limitations and a ridiculous loyalty to certain dogmas which are repugnant to one's intelligence. The contemplative alternative--the third one--is too unreal. Today it's impossible to withdraw from history. The hippies, as we will soon see, tried and failed. Religious orders are slowly dying. Competition, on the other hand, with its athletic-like challenge, in my opinion is closer to the human animal's sportive spirit, closer to the curious playful mammal that is very much a part of many people. Until now, this principal impulse--or is it strictly a cultural phenomenon--has produced the most imaginative and varied nation on this planet. Denying this is like trying to cover up the United States with your finger.

One final question about this matter. Is a collective rat race possible? In other words, is it possible for man to think of himself as part of humanity and for his struggle for success and recognition to lead toward collective undertakings? The communists have been working at it for a century, but curiously enough the only signs of success along these lines are coming from those strange monsters known as multinationals. Let's analyze the case of the hippies and why they dropped out of society.

HIPPIES AND CAPITALISM

Max Webber correctly pointed out that according to the Protestant ethic, the worship of productive work and the licit gain of wealth fit perfectly well with the Lutheran doctrine of predestination. To a certain degree those who were successful were successful because God so willed it. There was nothing sinful in the unlimited possession of material goods provided they were the result of a hard day's work. For three centuries the god "Work" remained enshrined on the high altar. The millionaire's son delivered papers. The senator's kid was a bag boy. Vagrancy was inscribed in the penal codes as a crime against society. Idleness was a case for scandal.

With this philosophy, the Yankees have built the most powerful nation in history. But at some point the religious origin which was the source of this conduct began to weaken. Christianity after twenty splendid centuries is headed toward its twilight. Protestantism, its final fruit, has begun to languish, and with it, its tremendous industrious energy. Scarcely fifteen years ago, a handful of dirty bearded youths offered the most heroic resistance to work of any description. Living was strictly a personal matter which didn't include debts to a society that awaited them with its smoking chimneys ready to swallow them up. They did away with the concept of "living together with others." Or at least they eliminated it as far as it was understood up until that time.

A few years ago among American youth there were millions of individuals willing to own absolutely nothing in exchange for being absolute masters of their own actions. Formerly, "being" was conditioned by "owning." Today self-esteem--the self-esteem of a growing sector of the population--is directly determined by the degree of individual freedom one possesses, inhibitions that are eliminated, restrictions that are removed, and man's finding total fulfillment without regard for the social "impediments" that surround him. Consequently, "owning," the magic fountain of progress, becomes a slippery instrument which enslaves, which alienates, to put it in today's jargon.

But the fabulous economic machinery of the United States was not dismantled. After centuries of incessant work, of struggle for progress, of advances, of science, of arduous sacrifice to achieve a happier civilization, a young man with a serious look and haughty manners strokes his bristly beard while he contentedly contemplates, plethoric with happiness, his filthy crusted feet. But this is not enough to neutralize the impulse to compete. The hippies attemped to drop out, but failed. The movement was a formidable spiritual adventure destined to fail. Let's take a look at the reasons.

Individualism and Competition

Scarcely a decade ago, the hippies--filthy with long matted hair, weird, pot-heads, generous, idealists--broke with the norm of behavior in the way they dressed and even in their outlook on the world. Where does this radically different attitude come from? How did this break come about? What phenomenon in the transmission of culture broke the continuity so spectacularly? Why are they so terribly different?

With the answer to this last question we can begin answering the others: because they lack a sense of competition. Because the instinct to compete readily visible in "the struggle to have a better life than anyone else," in the existence of athletic activities, in war--the nonpareil competitive event--has atrophied among the younger generation in countries where democracy and a consumer society coincide. Property acquired by grueling work seems to tire the mechanism that triggers competition. In addition, if the country has a system that respects liberty and the rights of her citizens, a "hippy"--in other words, any man without a sense of competition--will unfailingly emerge. In some relatively prosperous urban areas of Russia no hippies have emerged because the police state prevents it. An oppressive system prohibits the emergence of long-haired youth. The omnipotent Party would take upon itself to cut his hair, and put him in jail.

Ostensibly this conclusion contradicts the wide-spread criterion that hippies represent a strengthening of individualism. Or that by their extravagant clothes they try to reinfoce the "ego" which has been bewildered by the whirlwind of modern society What really happens is quite the contrary; the spirit of competition is the most formidable individualizer available to mankind. The hippies have deserted the herd of stampeding men struggling to obtain positions of leadership to join a flock which is placid and static--but a flock after all--where positions of leadership don't exist because they have lost all notion of movement. They have left the pack only to join the herd.

Viewed from this new perspective, the rest of their characteristics begin to take shape. For those who don't pursue any objective--no matter how useless or futile or foolish it might be--life is empty, absurd and an interminable succession of instants. That's why drugs--stupefacient and stupefying--fit in so well. Being alert is indispensable in a culture based on competition. Being alert would be senseless for those who have no goals. Filthy rags--renunciation of competition in dress--would necessarily have to be the uniform of the "non-competitive," in other words, those who don't compete. And what of our traditional vagabonds? They're nothing more than the humble forgotten ancestors of the ineffable hippy.

Where will all this take us? Nowhere. Humanity doesn't go anywhere. It moves in the direction indicated by its inner dialectic, but without having a predetermined destination. One thing is for sure. No matter what course humanity happens to be on, it's not going to be sidetracked by the hippy rebellion. Moreover, the hippies will disappear during this decade. The signs are very clear. After gaining a substantial following, the chaotic mass broke up into splinter groups. Thousands of young people formed "hippies colonies" where they live, sow, and eat in some kind of secular monastery. These social embryos will slowly begin revitalizing the spirit of competition among the bearded youth. Little by little the soap and water of metaphysical capitalism will penetrate the most remote pores of "hippieism." Then once again the herd will become a pack.

THE REAL HIDDEN FACE OF THE MOON

The spirit of competition doesn't operate only on the national level. There is sufficient evidence to support the theory that the lunar race was in its own way a competitive event.

They scratched her bald spot, harvested a hundred pounds or so of rock, spread around a dozen complex instruments, and started their trip back home. The moon--toothless and bald--remained immutable in its yellow somnambulism. Up to this point, the visible facts. The others are missing. The inner motivations--the spiritual rocket--that lift the human animal toward their satellite. We still don't know the impact that space adventures will have on the history of the adventurers. On all of us. On those that travel in the Apollo flights and on those that travel in modest antediluvian "jets." This division--astronauts vs. non-astronauts--signals an inedited chapter in history. Today, for the first time, a fissure in time is consciously emerging: the space crew with their outlandish uniforms and their damn little infallible machines live in the 21st century. The rest of us--almost the whole flock--live in our plain old ordinary present, petulant but at times delightful. Our lowly 20th century.

Actually any historic change can be explained by a mechanism of this sort: a group of individuals pivoting with one foot in the present and with the other blazing a trail in the future. Formerly the mechanism was a silent one. Nowadays they announce it with a count-down. Space-time-history is roaming all around sticking out its tongue at us. What's to be done about it? Some silly Marxists might suggest stating some sort of class struggle against the astronauts. Anything could happen. You never know. Meanwhile, they are "time-foreigners." It's time that we start talking about chronophobia. Men of the future already exist. They are here.

Moon, Earth and Geography

Let's not be excessively suspicious. As of now no one has gone to the moon in search of material goods. Nobody believes the silly idea of having an atomic base there to blow the other side to bits, especially no one in the Pentagon or the Red army. Individuals who refuse to accept the competition theory find this hypothesis helpful in coming up with a pedestrian justification, a simple explanation for the enormous investments that have been made. The race to the moon was nothing more than a race whose philosophy was that of any other race: to get to the goal before anyone else (because, without doubt, the important thing is to win, not to compete, in spite of what the Olympic Committee would have us believe).

First Krushchev--the chubby and cunning discus thrower--launched Sputnik. Eisenhower was playing golf. You can't run a country and play golf. The first race was won by Russia. Kennedy--who didn't play golf--launched his long distance challenge: a marathon to the moon. The Russians accepted the challenge. In the end, the two poles of present history converted part of their hostilities into competitive events. Along the way there appeared practices and inventions that allowed them to derive certain practical applications from the event, but the spirit of competition that propelled the colossi gathered strength from the mystery that is inherent in a competitive event. The position of leader would belong to the side that dominated technology with the greatest precision. To the side that more spectacularly evidenced ability to conjure up electronic apparitions. To the side that best cited the incantations of white magic. Since Sputnik, the ability to manipulate physics, mathematics, and science in general has been the measuring stick used to determine the power of empires.

The emergence of this phenomenon will have immediate consequences on the Earth's political boundaries. As the notion of conquest or territorial control loses its attraction, in other words, the old traditional imperialistic calling, the "zones of influence" and other anachronistic frauds will become less important. For many years now, from a military viewpoint, the "zones of influence" were totally inefficient, but they were retained as vestiges of the old system. Today this is becoming less attractive. The fetish for technology is replacing the fetish for the classic empire. In the end the Russians will realize that struggling to "communize" Angola is as idiotic as it is for someone else to struggle to keep Angola from being "communized." The game of cops and robbers which since the time of World War II has starred Gringos and tovarishes has become a scientific game.

This celestial alchemy has indirectly brought about another substantial change. In the old competition, military men were the heroes. Now the heroes are the scientists. The "demythicizing" of the military and the mythicizing of scientists is conducive to peace. It's preferable for our heroes to observe us with telescopes and not from watchtowers. That difference guarantees that our heads will stay on a little while longer.

The New Strategy of the Superpowers

During his time, Marx--from the shoulders of Hegel--presented his economic interpretation of history. Much later Ortega pointed to what he called a "martial interpretation" of human events. The Englishman Dawson has done something similar but from a religious angle. And so it is that man obsessed by the dynamic relationship of cause and effect has always tried to wrest the secrets from the mechanism that joins the various stages of development in man's age-old adventure.

Nowadays after examining the forces presently at work, it seems fitting to launch another hypothesis: the technological interpretation of history. For millenia the imperial calling of nations has been satisfied by the acquisition of territory and the subjugation of its inhabitants. The importance of an empire was measured by its size, population, and wealth. The prestige of a metropolis was weighed on an imperialistic scale. Hitler until 1945 and post-war Russia are good examples of this phenomenon.

We are just now beginning to catch a glimmer of the importance of an event that took place in 1969, the moon landing. The exact, precise mastery of technology placed a trembling biped on the selenite surface. Within twenty-four hours the United States grew in the eyes of the world to a size never attained by any other nation. Down below, Russia-- determined to keep her satellites within proper bounds--appeared to be some shaky version of the most remote past. At the very moment that empires were being built vertically towards space with armies of technicians, marshals in genetics, and admirals in computer science, the Soviets brutally maintained their "anachronistic" prestige by using bayonets and armoured tanks in defenseless Prague.

The mastery of technology, scientific dominion, will help remake the political boundaries of the world. A political orientation which postulates neo-isolationism has emerged in the United States. It has nothing to do with an egotistical concept of relationships between nations, but with an outlook totally different from the human phenomenon. Russia can have the whole "Third World." It's of no use to them. The alliance will be among nations capable of progress, fit for the technological sacrament. The other nations, those belonging to the "Third World," can legitimately head toward the "first world" or fall prey to some of the options offered by the communist Leviathan. The destiny of each nation will depend on its own efforts. As a matter of fact, Russia is the one who would benefit from abolishing her desire for a horizontal empire. What good will it do the Russians to be leader of some sub-world on the fringe of history? And what good will it do the Americans to play the role of world policemen and shed blood in futile endeavors which weaken her to the point of death?

In the American attitude toward events in Africa there is a great deal of isolationistic cunning. If the Russians want to take over Angola, that's their business. Deep down inside what they're really saying in Washington is that it would also be a good idea if they would burden themselves down with Rhodesia also. The nation that tries to maintain her expanding borders by force will jeopardize in doing so her chances to become technologically developed. In spite of everything, we can expect Russia to finally realize what the latest strategy is. If she carefully considers the new values now in force, if she discovers the subtleties of the game, maybe the human race will see better days, a brilliant period in which each nation's ambition will be to become a part of progress, research, and science in order to earn a prestigious place on the universal honor roll. A period in which empires grow toward the stars.

CAIN'S SPORT

Is America's neo-isolationism--for example, her inhibition in Portugal's affairs--an indication that she has renounced war? More likely it's an adjustment to the obvious fact that the excessive mastery of military technology is making military conflicts impossible. Ever since Cain slew Abel, men have sporadically squabbled. At some point, a simple blow became a full fledged war which ceased with the mushroom cloud at Hiroshima. The motive that inspired the Biblical fratricide is the same one that secretly, in our innermost depths, encourages war: the spirit of competition. Man is an inexorable competitor. In the broadest of terms, looked at from the simplification necessitated by the brevity of this essay, humanity emerges as a gigantic Olympus where most activities are no more than manifestations of this vigorous instinct to compete. "The struggle for a better life" is, in fact, "a struggle for a life better than the next guy's." The battle for fame, the ardent desire to excell, the indefatigable search for success are simply manifestations of competition. At times this instinct manifests itself symbolically. For example, when two human beings unquestionably and candidly beat the hell out of a tennis ball, or beat the hell out of each other in a boxing ring, or, completely out of breath, make a terrific effort to carry an inoffensive ball past the impenetrable defense of the opponents.

War, in its pristine origins, is another competitive event. A kind of basketball a la cannon ball. In another sense, basketball is a battle in which the fortress to be taken is a lowly ring attached to a rectangular board. In trying to justify war--any war--man has used enough ink to float a battleship. From the lofty religious war--with troops anointed by marvelous "god managers"--to the ideological war, every warlike event conceals its essential instinctive nature. But the instinct is not to fight but to compete. When man ceased practicing anthropophagy, war became a sport. As a matter of fact, it never was war, just as a fight between wild animals isn't war, but a vital process indispensable for ecological imperatives inflexibly dictated by nature.

Renouncing war, abandoning the uncomfortable alternative "communism vs. capitalism," or, if you prefer another cliché, "totalitarianism vs.

democracy," or if you prefer an absurdity, "West vs. East[1]," doesn't assume a radical change in man's attitudes but an inevitable adjustment in the race of very dangerous circumstances. What has happened is that the area of hostility has changed. After all, modern war is just a manifestation of our competitive spirit and not the result of secret aggressive tendencies. (Aggression-- in the physiological sense of the word, which is the only legitimate one--can't be found in decisions made in comfortable offices. But in those decisions we can indeed find a spirit of competition which is probably the most powerful combustible for the human motor.) Conflict will continue but on another level and with the forces regrouped in a different way. Now it's a matter of technological and scientific competition in which Europe and Japan will play separate roles.

For Latin America this new rhythm will seem strange and to a certain extent prejudicial. Our present relative importance will be reduced to something insignificant. At this stage we won't even be "booty" (to put it crudely and without sentimentality). Probably some of our politicians will still be carrying on in a prehistoric manner, in other words, subscribing to cold war rhetoric, but some day they'll realize that the scenery has been changed on them, that the play is a radically different one. We can assume that plans like the Alliance for Progress won't be repeated. That program was no more than a projectile of the cold war fired against the arsenal of communist propaganda. A dike of prosperity constructed to dam any flood of communism. Today it's of no vital importance to the United States if one or even several Andean countries embark upon the road to socialism. In Washington there rules an elf who recites by heart the pointless lines from Espronceda: "what difference does it make to the world that there is one cadaver more!" Especially if it's an underdeveloped cadaver, marginal as far as international consumption is concerned and one that's fasting instead of partaking of the technological sacrament. In the final analysis the bill for the funeral will wind up in some file in the Kremlin.

But something spectacular could happen. War could disappear from the face of the earth. Probably what will happen will be that "war" will be eliminated as an event in the competition. Not because man is better now, but because war is worse. In other words, atomic war has become humanly impossible. Since nuclear war cannot be controlled, the superpowers have opted to renounce it. There will be no nuclear competition because competitions are to be won, and no one can win competition of this sort. We are dealing with a new situation because until now every military discovery took as long to pulverize the enemy as it did to drag him out on the battlefield. Competition in order to be competition and fulfill its purpose must be carried out at full speed.

As long as atomic bombs stay chaste in their arsenals, conventional warfare with simple, rudimentary weapons isn't conceivable either. Therefore, man--that curious little competitive creature that refuses to give up his most treasured event--invented another sport, the technological race. Technology, the fetish-myth, is today's universal sport. Technological competition seems to be the substitute for military clashes. The race to the moon could have been termed the battle for the moon. In this new strategy, generals were replaced by scientists. A scientific event is won by setting foot on the moon or manipulating genes. War is no longer an exciting event.

THE IMPORTANCE OF MOUNT OLYMPUS

In a nation perpetually in competition like the United States, it's only natural for participation in sports to become an undeniable national cult. In that country when you reach a certain age, it's practically a crime not to participate in some sport. Later on in life, it will be a crime not to have a hobby. In a nation frenetically oriented toward action, idleness is the worst sin. We, on the other hand, have a different outlook. Competitive events are not one of the items appearing on the list of Hispanic-American priorities. This unfortunate mistake on the part of our governments has been around for quite some time. All these reflections are relevant to our failures in the Olympics, the failure of Latin America as a whole with the dubious exception of Cuba. In fact our disdain for competitive events, be they artistic or athletic, is part of our Hispanic culure. Our mother country is not acquainted with these matters either. One of the most illustrious absurdities committed by historians trying to explain Spain's decline as a first-rate international power is to persist in her "impractical," "chivalrous," "romantic" nature. It never crossed Cervantes' mind that his madman from La Mancha would be a marvelous excuse for Spain's shunning the bulk of her historic responsibilities. Very often the word "quixotic" has been used where "dumb" would have done very nicely.

A "competitive event" can be anything that doesn't have a practical purpose. They don't provide us with anything to eat. Art on the one hand is creation and on the other competition. It produces spiritual pleasures closely related to what the soccer player experiences when he executes a well-aimed kick. The points, whether they're made by Siqueiros or Pelé, are aimed first at Siqueiros and Pelé's own personal satisfaction and then at generating enthusiasm among the spectators. We should make a note of these two words: satisfaction and enthusiasm. We'll get back to them later.

At first glance, it seems that it's of no consequence that Germans run faster than Paraguayans. If this be the case, then it's preferable to invest money in a sewage system rather than in some Spanish speaking Indian who can "negotiate" the hundred meter dash in nine seconds. The same applies regarding our painters, writers, pianists, and sculptors. When the time comes to request official aid, budgetary support, they have to compete with illiteracy, malnutrition, arms or malaria. And, of course, they don't get their slice of the pie. Our states aren't interested in becoming "athlete factories." It's the same whether dealing with muscles or brains. Competitive events, be they in art or in sports--as we've already said--can't be eaten. So there at the edge of our society lies an enormous amount of talent--or biceps--that goes to waste without ever having known the taste of success. Let's be frank. The only Olympic record never broken is the one set by the idiot who declared that the important thing was not to win, but to compete. The only important thing is to win, because without winning competition has no meaning, and losing, which for an athlete or an artist is to be surpassed by others, causes deep frustration. Profound frustration.

To diminish the importance of victory or defeat is to disregard man's true nature. It seems that the only ones hurt by the lack of official support are those who participate in competition. Who else besides them is hurt by the lack of an energetic policy which sponsors the arts and games? The whole nation. That's who. As it turns out, competition not only involves a few people in some far away place smearing paint on a canvas, throwing javelins, or composing sonatas. Competition is also the entire nation gaining satisfaction via the creations of her artists or becoming enthusiastic because of her muscular heroes. In other words it's a matter of nourishing the nation with emotions that its citizens share with each other. It's quite obvious; "community" results from having things in common. It's not because of an accident of geography, but because they share a common way of life. If you want to promote national pride, give people emotions they can cling to and contemporary heroes with whom they can identify. Provide the people with victories won by their fellow countrymen, and they will make them their own through an inevitable psychological projection. What is enthusiasm--and here is where I come back to the key words--if it's not the spectators appropriating the joy of the players? A goal and the satisfaction of having made it belong not only to the player who made it but to the fans who make it theirs by breaking into unanimous applause.

Doesn't everyone in Guatemala feel a kind of veneration for Asturias[2] ? The Nobel prize of the author of El Señor Presidente is shared in some way by all Guatemalans. How can we Latin Americans--undone, without technological accomplishments to exhibit, without well organized societies, without strong economies, without scholars, without respectable political structures--prevent skepticism and disenchantment from becoming rampant? The Latin-American citizen feels more like a victim than a part of his nation. If countries more heterogeneous than ours, the United States for instance, have been able to ride out wild storms, it has been because of that feeling of "collective participation" that its citizens possess. (All the Gringos have stock invested in their country. The only ones who didn't were the racial minorities, and fortunately they have now begun to acquire their share.)

It's inexcusable for a modern day government official to be ignorant in psychology. In order to demand patriotism, nationalism, and another half dozen isms that belong to the sphere of pathos, you have to start by nourishing the emotional world of the governed with something more than ancient symbols which have been weakened by time. It's criminal to ignore the sewers, bread, and schools, but it's stupid to overlook the arts and sports. We must rescue the competitive spirit from the superficial level to which mental laziness has relegated it and return it to the areas of our most desperate urgencies.

NOTES

[1] As far as history is concerned, the "East" hasn't existed for a long time. Communism, the prayer-book devoted to the saints of progress, to terrestrial felicity, and to equality, is the most western of the dogmas, even though it's subscribed to by Koreans and Chinese.

[2] Miguel Angel Asturias. Contemporary Guatemalan poet and novelist, author of _El Señor Presidente_ and winner of the Nobel Prize for literature.

VI

AMERICAN VIOLENCE

BETWEEN LAW AND ORDER

The United States projects an image of violence. From the European viewpoint cities like New York are practically firing ranges. The movies and television with their naive sagas about gangsters, policemen, Indians, cowboys, and, as of late, karate, make an appreciable contribution to this image. I don't doubt that they magnify the image of violence. Apparently America is destroying itself in street fights. Is it true? It's true that the crime rate is up, but that, of course, is not a serious problem. It's primarily a problem in certain urban areas where ghettos exist. And the difficulty in solving it stems from the fact that official violence, the violence of the state--as revolutionaries like to put it--has been decreasing. The American police force, unlike the criminals, can't rely on unlimited action. The alleged criminal, until proven guilty, has at his disposal all the rights guaranteed by law. Even after he has been found guilty, any kind of procedural error during the investigation is all it takes to set him free. The arrest must be carried out according to the law. The Americans' Sadducean passion for defending legality sometimes leads them to injustice. In essence this is right. In a state ruled by law, if you have to choose between legality--the law, which is a written text on which social conduct is based--and justice, which is an abstract value, it's preferable to opt for legality. The American interpretation of law tends to follow these lines. It probably indirectly helps perpetuate certain groups operating beyond the reach of the law, but most citizens have a clear concept of the limits of their own individual rights.

A consideration of another sort also enters the picture. Are the people who live in these urban areas which developed in the 20th century really "violent"? What was it like before? I'm of the opinion that it was much more risky in days gone by because in the old days it was customary to wear side arms or firearms. Or both. The countryside was full of bandits and official violence was carried out without batting an eye. Torture was part of official procedure. American communities more often than not had no jail, but wrongdoers were punished in the public stocks or by the strange humiliation of being tarred and feathered.

Probably our 20th century has seen a great decrease in unlawful conduct or--seen from the other side--a considerable increase in individual safety. Perhaps it's incorrect to assume that several decades of relative civil tranquility were proof of a permanent civilized society. It's extremely difficult--using Manhattan as an example--for ten million human beings to live together on a stretch of asphalt without violence breaking out.

Of course, there are means of eliminating violence, but all of them lead to the restriction of individual rights. By using preventive arrests, torture, electronic listening devices or arbitrary interrogation, the rate of <u>public</u> crime would drop, but the other variety, official violence, would rise. And this variety of violence more often than not becomes more annoying than the extra-official variety.

For what it's worth, it should be remembered that "individual safety" is the product of idealism. Another cultural abstraction. One of the most easily proved facts of nature is that life--everything that lives, eats, multiplies and grows--exists in a perpetual state of danger. Those strange intuitive defense mechanisms that are part of all living beings are nothing more than evidence of the risks inherent in the process of staying alive. However, this assertion is of little consolation to a citizen of flesh and blood. Man, especially 20th century man, desires a <u>safe</u> cultural environment. Violence among other things terrifies him because he has been educated to live together in peace and harmony with his fellow men and not to defend himself. He doesn't even attempt to lucidly interpret acts of violence. A recent case, Patricia Hearst, is a good example of America's shock when confronted with a kind of violence practically unknown in that country: revolutionary violence.

PISTOL PACKING PATTY

The <u>Gringos</u> who scarcely have any sort of revolutionary fauna haven't the foggiest idea what went on in that girl's little head. They don't understand how nor why the princess changed into a witch; how Snow White became La Pasionaria. So they did something very rational and made up a story about brainwashing, insurmountable fear, and temporary insanity. Bull!

Patricia Hearst went to war because she damn well wanted to. And she damn well wanted to because it's much more interesting to be a revolutionary than a millionaire or a terrorist than a pharmaceutical salesman. Five intense minutes in the life of a PLO guerrilla is worth more than half a century in a bookkeeper's soft life.

During the hours of anguish which she spent locked in a closet, Patricia Hearst became aware of the enormous difference between going to a cocktail party and robbing a jewelry store. There's no substitute for those intense minutes with the machine-gun, the victim, and the danger. The spurt of adrenaline that electrified her, her pounding heart, her sweaty hands, her intolerable urge to urinate, the whole repertoire of energetic biological response to revolutionary action filled her gew-gaw Dior soul with new life.

Patricia Jekyll became Tania Hyde for more or less the same reasons Al Capone had for not opening a pizza parlor. Because it's infinitely more fun to live outside the law than within its boring perimeter.

In our society there is an old masochistic tendency to look for the cause of the crime outside the personality of the criminal and to forget how much satisfaction, how much sheer enjoyment there is in committing certain acts punishable by law. In this flat, orderly and inoffensive world, being a delinquent is one of the few adventures left. There are no more abysses, giants, or monsters. (There never were but people searched for them, which is the same thing.)

Gold is discovered with complicated electronic devices. Lions now lie around in cages, and the only thing tigers are good for is providing coats for a few elegant ladies. The only adventure within reach is subversion. In this world of computers what's left for those unfortunate souls with adventurous spirits? Either they become part of a conspiracy or contract some kind of gall bladder disorder. There's no other alternative within reach. How many Trotskyites have died of sadness because they had to punch IBM cards?

Patricia Hearst had the time of her life. A

group of crazy adventurous fanatics--drunk on words and adrenaline--kidnapped her in the midst of the boring quiet of a California afternoon. But they also kidnapped her imagination. They aroused in Patricia Hearst, who was bored from writing checks and reading nonsense, a sense of adventure. And Tania, who is more important than Patricia, emerged, and she went forth to hunt lions, kill giants, and defend some God knows what "symbionese" absurdity.

Leon de Greiff, the great Colombian poet, wrote the following sad poem: "I would exchange my life for a deck of cards/or for two tiny holes/at my temples--through which the plethora, all the weariness, all the horror that I have stored in my wine skins/could escape in grey pus!/In any case my life is already lost."

Patricia's life was pointless because she was a good girl and had clean fingernails. Is that insanity? No. Revolutionaries are not insane. Adventurers are not insane. However, they do lose their sense of reality, but only as an excuse for undertaking adventure. The Symbionese Liberation Army or Guevara's little wars were not created by madmen. They were simply men determined to make the most of their lives. People unwilling to die of boredom in the office of some wheezing lawyer.

People who talk about the "sacrifices" made by revolutionaries don't have the slightest idea what they're saying. The adventurer, the figure found in epics, even enjoys his own death. Why do so many revolutionaries come from the delinquent sector of society? Why do so many revolutionaries-- the Maquis, for example--become delinquents after a war? Because animals of action, adventurous temperaments, end up making no distinction between a Nazi soldier and a bank guard. Their ethics get very blurred when faced with the inexorable vice of action.

In the end Miss Hearst lost her judgment, not the judgment claimed by her psychiatrist all bogged down in his Freudian medical rhetoric, but the other , the one concerning punishment. And it wouldn't make any difference if the perplexed jurors had found her innocent. One day, all decked out in her glad rags having a martini, she would have remembered Tania. Then she would have become nostalgic for her beret and pistol. She would have shed a tear and eaten another horrible caviar canape. And that night in her dreams she would have relived the unforgettable nightmare. Severe punishment! Terrible punishment!

But her case, far from shedding some light on the dark zone of the motivations of most revolutionaries, has helped cloud the issue. Of course, there are some trite theoreticians who prefer to see in these insane acts the emergence of some kind of redeemer conscience. That's not how it is at all. Revolution, better yet, revolutionary insurrection is almost a sportive phenomenon. Let's take a look.

FIRE FOUR SHOTS

The nihilists were right. Four shots fired at the mob are worth more than all the political theories in the world. At least they're worth more if it's a matter of creating enthusiasm. The periodic slaughter with which Jews and Arabs have been amusing themselves for some years now and the acts of the ETA[1] are cases in point. The blurry origins of the conflict have faded into the background. For some time now the only thing that counts is destroying the enemy in the most spectacular way possible. Action, the mere action of certain men grown accustomed to war, is what keeps the tension of the struggle alive. Ideology, rights, justice, and other ethereal abstractions are mere pretexts. The ultima ratio of entanglement is the shots that are fired. What I'm trying to say is that the shots are not instruments of any kind of entelechy but an end in themselves. As a matter of fact, you can't expect anyone to become fanatical simply by being acquainted with a tome as boring as Das Kapital or to crash through barricades because he has memorized delirious verses from the Torah or the Koran. The texts--allow me this puerility--are the pretexts. What inspires action and sacrifice is action and sacrifice themselves in an uncontrollable vicious circle.

What seduces the ordinary man in the streets--the obtuse superficial individual--is not the reasons that justify the action, but the skill, audacity, and "neatness" with which the action is carried out. Terrorists, no matter what color they are, have an intuitive understanding of those mysterious innermost parts of human psychology, and they draw on them when the time comes to recruit their clientele.

As an example, let's consider the recent activities of the Tupamaros.[2] The Tupamaros aroused the "admiration" of half a continent. The goals of the group were ignored because no one cared about what they were trying to achieve. The wave of goodwill resulted from the audacity they used to carry out their attacks. It came from the spectacle. How can anyone pretend that a border dispute--a pure legalistic invention--a doctrine, or any other entity of fiction (of exclusively verbal make-up) can electrify the masses? Action or the ritual symbols of action are what fanaticize. The Internationale and not Das Kapital is electrifying. The military parade, the spectacle, what's actually going on out there and can be "spectated" and related to with blood and muscle and life and death are what rouse people to rebellion. Humanity doesn't give a damn about "surplus value."

From the above--if my hypothesis is correct--it can be deduced that guerrilla warfare belongs to the realm of sports. The enthusiasm and repudiation that it causes are close relatives of the fanaticism found among sports fans. The physical expertise of the individual who plants a bomb is admired with the same openness that a goal made from a difficult angle is. Violence--the epitome of action--provokes instinctive adhesion. This phenomenon--which for the sake of brevity we call the "Robin Hood syndrome"--has one fatal peculiarity. It's within the reach of any visionary. When Feltrinelli grew tired of editing tons of useless Marxist papers, he became a terrorist. Guevara, after writing about communist economy and ethics for a number of years--the old Argentinean did write well, although with a marked predilection for foolishness--decided to provide the victim for the Bolivian adventure. Action, sheer action--St. Ignatius, St. Teresa, Lenin, Mao--changes the world and polarizes in phobia and "philias" man's spirit.

Needless to say, I'm writing this with a certain amount of regret. It would be preferable at this stage in man's psychological evolution--the history that he has worn like a pair of pants for the last twenty thousand years--to appraise action in relation to the goals being sought, but obviously that's not how it is. We're still closer to the horde than we imagine. In fact it took our hairy ancestors millions of years to finally identify the qualities of the leader most fit to organize that long difficult trek to survival. I suppose it will take us a long time to rid ourselves of the genes that carry that heroic trait. Meanwhile, I regret to say, it is still more effective to empty a revolver than write a book.

THE RIGHT TO TORTURE

The increasing frequency with which these revolutionary groups are appearing has caused individual and collective safety in modern nations to be restricted. Consequently, repression, official violence, leads back to practices that supposedly had been banished from our society. Today torture is a brutal reality in some of the Spanish speaking countries.

Jean Cau, the brilliant French writer, in a dramatic report published in the European press, affirms, without hiding his own horror, that the modern state can only defend itself against terrorist action by torturing those who have been arrested. In other words, if it's a matter of disbanding a group of conspirators, the only effective way is to pull the threads until the knots appear. "Pulling the threads" is a metaphor meaning kicking testicles; pulling out fingernails, hair, and pieces of skin; applying electrodes to the ears and genitals; yanking out teeth and another dozen barbarities that would send chills up the spines of Masoch and Sade.

The dilemma is terrible. The first thing that comes to mind is to say that instead of wiping out the conspirators, the causes of the conspiracy should be eliminated: put an end to social and political injustices. But this, even though it's right, won't solve the problem. It's a demagogic and idiotic reply. The heart of the matter is that the juridical structure of a democratic state is equipped only to deal with isolated delinquents who are more or less docile, for example the civilized pickpockets in London who would never dream of carrying arms as long as the bobbies use only clubs or whistles. (Apparently, kids aren't the only ones who play cops and robbers.) As with almost everything, breaking the law--and sanctioning it--forms part of a complicated ritual that, if violated, becomes a big mess. When crime becomes organized, when it becomes a sect and creates its own <u>modus operandi</u> on the periphery of police jurisdiction, the state loses its repressive efficiency. London can deal with violent Jack the Ripper but it can't handle the IRA and the Protestant antagonists. The United States, subjected more and more to the vigilance of civil liberties organizations in dealing with the Black Muslims, the Black Panthers, and the Cosa Nostra, has lost the effectiveness which allowed her to terminate the KKK. In Latin America brutal regimes such as those in Brazil, Haiti, and Cuba can eliminate any kind of belligerent opposition by skinning prisoners alive until they learn where the nucleus of the conspiracy lies. Until Uruguay began using these very same methods, the country was in a state of perpetual and defenseless fear.

If the dilemma is real, then the honorable thing is to examine it carefully. If we accept the hypothesis that the <u>only</u> effective weapon to combat terrorism is official counterterrorism--torture on the part of the police and renunciation of judicial principles found in democratic states--we come across the unpleasant evidence that in trying so hard to combat the enemy we have ended up imitating him. The first unavoidable contradiction. Someone will probably say that I'm looking for metaphysical characteristics where they don't exist, but just the opposite is the case. The problem is metaphysical. A democratic state and its enemies are having an essentially metaphysical dispute. For three centuries the political conflict has boiled down to the interpretation of what is just and what is not just, what can or should be sacrificed in the search for justice and the place that justice should have in our system of values. The unfortunate part is that the discrepancies in these metaphysical disputes are resolved by guillotines, firing squads, insane asylums and other instruments of political "persuasion."

Second contradiction. Let's assume that brutal repression not allowed by law is authorized to combat some emergency situation. What limitations will apply? Will suspects be tortured or only those who are obviously guilty? Who will make the decision? The torturer? Can we confide in the "good judgment" of a barbarian capable of castrating one of his fellow citizens? There was a time, long before the era of Human Rights, long before Man and Humanity, etc. were written with capital letters, that torture was a legitimate part of the judicial process. The Inquisition, for example, had several degrees of torture: whipping, the rack, asphyxiation, etc. Confessions extracted in this fashion were considered valid and normal. The prosecutors supervised the torture, and there was even a kind of manual of procedure written by Institor at the behest of the Pope entitled <u>Malleus Maleficarum</u>, or <u>The Witch's</u>

Hammer. Can the reader justify a backward step of three hundred years in the evolution of law? Can the reader justify kangaroo courts, investigators who resort to torture, and sacrificing painstaking and subtle advances that have been made for the cause of Human Rights?

Now let's take a look at the other side of the coin. How can a democratic state successfully fight secret organizations which operate out of reach of its repressive resources without betraying its very essence? Is it right--and here again we have the inexorable dilemma of justice--to put into practice certain repulsive means to obtain certain objectives just as the enemy does? Or should the state remain faithful to the principles that support it even at the risk of lapsing into chaos?

What is the solution? It seems to me that if I were to answer the question I would be depriving the reader of his painful and irrevocable duty to meditate, arrive at conclusions and maintain them honestly. I personally believe that these methods should never be used under *any* circumstances. Civilized government, in order not to degenerate into some kind of *Mafia*, should begin by limiting the amount of violence it permits itself to use. Even so, the matter, as we will see, is diabolically complicated.

POWER AND THE POWER TO KILL

In the Kafkaesque senatorial hearing concerning Watergate a perplexed congressman asked one of Nixon's aids if the President could have someone killed. Of course, he was referring to extrajudicial crimes and those occurring in peacetime. He was referring to slitting throats outside the mechanism where such things are legitimate, correct and at times plausible. He was referring to killing disquieting foreign colleagues, dangerous leaders, spies, or any enemy who commits his dreadful acts at a safe distance from the domestic penal code. Faced with this question posed with ethical horror, Nixon's aid smiled ironically and refused to answer.

To accept that a head of state can "have someone killed" much in the fashion of some Sicilian *Mafioso* is monstrous. Now we begin to see some of the perverse subtleties of this diabolic situation. Would the assassination of Hitler before 1939 have been a condemnable act? Wouldn't a few timely drops of cyanide--originality is not necessary--have prevented forty million deaths? Was the assassination of Trujillo--where foreign intervention was clearly present--a reproachable act? Trujillo had already attempted to kill Betancourt, the president of Venezuela. The next targets could have been Muñóz Marín, Kennedy, or Figueres. How can we possibly draw well defined ethical lines involving a question so painfully subjective? Within Stalin's logical schemes, assassinating Trotsky was almost a patriotic undertaking, and Roman Mercader was an archangelic citizen. How can you talk of what is right or wrong when you are talking about a crime--or what have you--that is carried out based on political, philosophical and ethical suppositions that are absolutely relative? Those on the other side called the "brave-heroism-of-our-soldiers" genocide. The Spanish statue of Marshall Weyler always amazes me (in a melancholy way). Weyler was a visionary; at the end of the past century he invented concentration camps to crush the Cuban insurrection.

Now that's precisely what power is: to be able to kill on a greater or lesser scale. I suspect that the political structure that we men have built is no more than a means to help us escape from the scythe of the leader. The most powerful man is the one who has the most freedom to make heads roll. Those incredible Caribbean leaders--Trujillo, Duvalier, Castro--who can annihilate an enemy by lifting their little fingers accumulate more power than those who head the big powers, for the latter are subject to the restriction and red tape of the modern bourgeois state. In the complex psychology of those who rule, atomic arsenals and enormous armies carry little weight compared with the power over life and death that one of these tyrants holds. By invoking certain magical terrifying abstractions--"national security," "sovereignty," "order," "law," "justice," "fatherland," and other abracadabra words--any petty statesman legitimizes bombing his fellowmen, devastating a district, exterminating an alien racial group, and annihilating mutineers.

But we always talk about indiscriminate assassinations within reach of any poor devil with a scepter. To determine who holds Grand Power--with glowing capital letters-we must see who has the ability to carry out discriminate assassinations. An orgasm of authority isn't reached by killing Man--also with a capital letters--but by killing a Trotsky, a Ben Barka, or a Jesús Galíndez; by eliminating <u>that</u> adversary without sparing any of the circumstances that augment the seriousness of the crime: premediation, aggravated assault, malice, aforethought, etc.

POLICE 1984

Violence, aggression, repression and other subjects treated in this chapter have provoked a reaction from one of the most influential and dangerous American psychologists. There on the loose, selling by the millions a frightening book entitled <u>Beyond Freedom and Dignity</u> is the psychologist "behaviorist" Skinner. With the demolition equipment of the behaviorist--a bunch of implacable and exact scholars, unpardonable renegades from humanistic ambiguity--Dr. Skinner has formulated an hypothesis: in spite of all the warning signs, human society still is progressively deteriorating and is inexorably doomed. Pollution, over-population, inhuman urban complexes, a rise in the crime rate all point to the catastrophic end of the species <u>Homo sapiens</u>. The human has had it unless we try a behavioristic experiment on a universal level. It has nothing to do with "educating" hard-head human beings, a measure he considers useless at this stage of the game. It's a matter of changing behavioral patterns by methodically manipulating his cultural habitat. It's a matter of defining in pragmatic terms what's best and favorable for our species and then conditioning human psychology to obtain these objectives. Just as a Kaffir raised in London behaves like a British gentleman and not like a Kaffir, so will the behaviorists' <u>new man</u> act in accordance with the hierarchy of values that have been engraved on him and in accordance with the ideals that he has been given to breathe in his cultural atmosphere. In Skinner's judgment, this colossal manipulation is justifiable not only because of the imperative to survive, but because, after all, the mere act of existing in a culture supposes subjection to certain values, myths, and dogmas that <u>also</u> determine, limit, and dictate our behavior. As a result--according to Skinner--we will not be <u>less</u> free in his experiment but we will be correctly "free."

In order to establish his "happy World"--and I don't mean to be ironic about something that is very serious--those who run the show will rely on the only means recognized by the behaviorists as being effective: reinforcement. Positive reinforcement (some kind of recompense) to reward "right" behavior and negative reinforcement (some kind of punishment) to show disapproval of "wrong" behavior. Right or wrong--as I have already said--will be determined by what is good for the species and by criteria more biological than theological. (In the final analysis biology is subject to the bondage of ethics, which in itself is revealing.)

Up to this point, it's been all Skinner. Summarizing two hundred pages in twenty lines is highly abusive, but at least the basics have been pointed out. Now for a different twist let's analyze what our psychologist has said. First, let's pass judgment on the hypothesis. Are our lives really degenerating? What point of reference are we to use? Pericles' Athens, the paleolithic Transvaal, or Teddy Roosevelt's New York? Is our species really in the process of being wiped out? Unquestionably unquestionably? our existences are filled with tensions not present two hundred years ago, but I'm not so sure that our species is headed for a catastrophe. Of course, it's a different world as it always has been ever since "man" was some scared little animal wandering about the savannas sleeping in caves, but simply because it's <u>different</u> it's not better or worse. Ever since we joined the adventure of culture we started out on a trajectory without a fixed destination, a trajectory which pitted us against nature. Culture is precisely that notion-of-being-on-the-way, that sensation of "trajectory" without our efforts being fully justified. (Those are the risks you run when you invent yourself; there's no way of stopping it without collective suicide.) In other words, Skinner's premise might not be right. Realizing that prehistoric man survived the glaciers, epidemics, and predators in spite of the defenselessness of his anatomy frightens me more than the rising crime rate or the present level of pollution. Our species, packed in small concrete cubicles, breathing carbon monoxide, coming to blows with each other every time we get a chance, is safe. At least for the time being.

And what about the new custom-made psycho-cultural habitat made for the scientifically manipulated man? Skinner has forgotten an extremely important aspect: that our present psycho-cultural habitat is subject to perpetual changes. It is false to suppose that it does not closely correspond to the "interests" of our species. Or isn't there an enormous distance between Victorian England and the Beatles' England? How is Skinner going to replace those illusive dynamic malleable values which always interplay with characteristics of the society of which they are a part? Skinner has forgotten that the Kaffir not only becomes a Londoner but that he changes London, he molds her millimeter by millimeter to meet his (biological?) need to innovate and be adventurous. Not everything--and may the implacable behaviorists pardon me--is subject to the immutable mechanics of physical laws.

And now I'm left with the worst fear of all. I agree that all cultures contain a changing system of coercion, repression and conditioning. We are not as free as we would like to be. We don't have all the dignity we would like to have. But who is to determine the priority of values, set common goals, design beneficial bridles for the human race? Scientists? Why not poets? (After all, Breton's motto, the motto of the surrealists, was "change life.") At this stage of the game, anyone saying he possesses the truth deserves to be laughed at, but it's no laughing matter. Plans to manufacture new men are almost always nullified by exterminating the old ones. It's quite simple. When Dr. Skinner's little white mice refuse to run through the paths of his merry maze, the only possibility left will be to take a broom to them. Our 20th century has already produced enough "jailers of noble causes," enough "assassins of good intentions" to run the risk of incubating another batch. And what really makes me uneasy is that I suspect there's nothing comparable to the wrath of a behavioral scientist whose experiments have failed.

NOTES

[1] ETA. Basque terrorist organization favoring Basque independence.

[2] Tupamaros. Uruguayan terrorist organization.

VII

SEX IN THE USA

USA: THE PERMISSIVE SOCIETY

The adjective permissive is not entirely precise. Society is something like a catalogue of forbidden items in which man will fatally acquiesce. If the catalogue is long and detailed, society is totalitarian. The West, headed by the United States and England, for some time now has been yanking pages out of the catalogue. Society is becoming more permissive. More things are permitted.

In Biblical mythology it's curious that the symbol is so obvious. Adam and his rib were different from the other creatures because they were arbitrarily forbidden to eat a certain fruit. From that point on any kind of association--society--has had a list of prohibitions which are more or less arbitrary; however when the term "permissive" is applied to society, it doesn't mean that the penal code has been reduced. It almost always refers to a greater tolerance in sexual matters. In other words, a permissive society is one that rejects ancient prohibitions concerning the human animal's sexual behavior. One that has relinquished its obligations in the realm of moral transgressions. One that simply ignores what goes on south of the navel.

In the catalogue of forbidden items, it's surprising to note that the lion's share has to do with sexual prohibitions. Christianity is responsible for this. For centuries the obsession of Christianity has been sex. Those medieval councils where learned men debated the sex of angels or the sinful state of women's underwear stand out as the most illustrious episodes in the universal annals of nonsense. Celibacy, chastity, virginity became the ghosts that were to haunt Christian consciences for centuries. It's interesting to note that the New Testament--Jesus--scarcely deals with matters of sexual proscription. When that small sect of heterodox Jews ended up inheriting the structures of the Roman Empire, when Christianity became a special society, that's when the fear of sex began. It's not an exaggeration to say that the great debates that have taken place within Christendom have been limited to sex: the Immaculate Conception of Mary, celibacy

(Luther), divorce (Henry VIII), the pill (half the world).

This aberration of the Church (_ab-_ , from + _errare_, to wander; deviation from a right, customary, prescribed, natural course) resulted in a repressive society as far as sexual behavior was concerned. In 19th century England clitorectomies were performed on women suspected of masturbation. And the legs on furniture were covered because they could be perversely associated with sex. Until the beginning of the 60's the specters of sex were still operating quite effectively. It was at that prodigious moment--ten instantaneous years!--that the non-totalitarian countries began to lose that centenary rigidity. Society--well, a part of it--became permissive.

And now we find ourselves on the threshold of a permissive society. Grandmothers go straight from mass to see _Oh, Calcutta!_ Artists and writers openly declare themselves bisexual (which biologicaly is as absurd as saying that they are bicephalus and quadruped). In Miami, New York and San Francisco there is a proliferation of sex-shops, small aseptic shops selling strange items "that increase the couple's pleasure." Homosexuality has ceased being a blemish and has become a peculiarity, something like being cross-eyed or left-handed. Man is no longer judged by his own particular sexual conduct. Sex has been withdrawn from the field of ethics.

What consequences will this permissive society possibly have on the human race? There are those who think it's an indication of the final cataclysm. To start with, it seems to me that the more a society eliminates prohibitions and obligations, the more hospitable it becomes. To me China, Albania, and Cuba--where everything that's not prohibited is obligatory--seem more like straightjackets than countries. It's odd that countries that are officially atheistic are the ones that adhere most firmly to a kind of theological morality. But it's not a contradiction. Totalitarianism consists of pruning the individual for the (supposed) benefit of the group while permissive society, by eliminating prohibitions--apparently-- greatly increases the realm of personal decisions. In other words, it reinforces individualism. Nevertheless, in bourgeois democracies Marxist leftists, when not in power, cry out for the victory of a permissive society, but once in power they prove to be unyielding partisans of genital law and order. Remember how Nikita, that joker from the Ukraine, railed against an innocent show of cancan dancers?

Naturally a certain degree of agressive exaggeration on the part of the initiates was to be expected during the debut of this new morality which is less rigid and less inhibited. But a certain singer's triumphant self-proclamation of her bisexuality and the gratuitous nudity of the "living theater" are no less grotesque than covering the legs of a piano for reasons of modesty. Once the commotion of this first stage is over I hope this exhibitionistic foolishness will come to an end. Apparently what won't disappear will be the adscription of sex to ideological confrontations. Let's see.

American Sex Is Not in the Middle

It should be, but it's not. It's on the left. In a fair fight, if there were something reasonably logical on this planet, sex would be equidistant from the two extremes. Nevertheless, it has almost never been that way. Scarcely a few centuries ago when Calvin was anathematizing from his refuge in Switzerland, sex was on the right. In other words, those showing more tolerance in sexual matters were the Catholics, the Establishment at that time. During the Renaissance, the Roman Curia was so merry and sensual that sensitive souls like Luther and Erasmus were scandalized by the licentious habits of the festive cardinals.

Today--or to be more exact, since the beginning of this century--the left has become the champion of sexual tolerance. In the United States, where the phenomenon is absolute, magazines and other "spicy" publications--many times bordering on the coarsest kind of pornography--alternate praises of Brezhnev with photos of spectacular women in the nude. On the other hand, those who shake their heads and demand less explosive practices and invoke the remote past of the passengers on the Mayflower are the most conservative elements in the country, which in the most common and unimaginative political nomenclature is called "the right." Patriotism for that sector of the population means raising the neckline to chin level and rejecting with all their might premarital sex. It would be interesting for Reagan, Wallace, and Billy Graham, if only for the sake of disconcerting their adversaries, to call for a shorter miniskirt, the legalization of marijuana, and greater sexual freedom for adolescents. But this could never happen. The right is going through a crisis and consequently their norms of morality are also.

The price paid by something that has been in vogue is ceasing to be in vogue. Tomorrow, when today's vociferous left becomes the hated "establishment," when it becomes the element in power, then sex will probably once again become the patrimony of the right. I hope some day we will decide to leave sex out of our officious squabbles. Right in the strategic middle where the Creator assigned it. Perhaps the new sexual morality which is now making its debut, by demythicizing, will aid in removing sexual conduct from the social arena. That's probably what will happen.

THE NEW SEXUAL MORALITY: A WORLD WITHOUT INHIBITIONS

Okay, it's absurd to deny it. We have witnessed the most radical change in human sexual conduct. In scarcely a decade the most formidable taboos were shot to pieces. Good and evil as determined by the norms of Christian ethics began to become blurry. They were confused. They were mixed. It seems that the combative generation of the 70's shouted for absolute sexual freedom until they were hoarse. In Freudian jargon this means that inhibition of the libido imposed by culture will weaken and finally disappear. Finally, after an extremely long battle, human beings who no longer associate their sexual activities with the concept of good and evil will emerge. Sex will be withdrawn from the area of ethics. In fact this is what Marcuse proposes (Marcuse is an equation of Marx plus Freud minus Fromm). Freud assumed that culture was the result of energy accumulated from the repressive forces that society imposed on the libido. The vicious triangle (why not?) was formed by the fact that man flourished only within a culture and culture in turn subjected the human being to the repression of his instincts, forces that constantly created modifications in his own culture. But now a man has raised his head above the triangle. His face is bearded and his matted hair is long. Everything seems to indicate that the observation made by Marcuse--who is a good observer but not a philosopher--is valid. The younger generation has less inhibitions and perhaps will be successful in casting them all off where sex is concerned. If this be the case and if Freud's hypothesis is valid, can culture survive in a world free from repression of the libido? Marcuse, an optimist, thinks so. Personally, I've always thought the Freudian hypothesis was a poetic pack of lies.

The Magic Pill

The pill was the detonator of the sexual explosion. The jolt fragmented what was formerly a monolith into three distinct worlds: sex, maternity and "legitimate" union. Rid of previous difficulties, it's now possible for a couple to enjoy, shall we call it, sportive love. Love without embarrassing consequences or without an "honest" purpose. Immediate pleasure is being sought; the gratification of an impulse; biological copulation. Reprisals, reprimands, or intent to marry are nonexistent. Just plain old sex. Once maternity is effectively controlled, the age of the couples will gradually be reduced until society and hormones coincide. When puberty begins, so will sex. It was absurd to think that nature had made a mistake. Adolescents will love each other. (Can anyone love more tenderly than two children?) Maternity--and this is the beautiful and meritorious aspect--will be a willful act, by free choice and not by biological mischance. A child will be desired, and it will be because his parents wanted it that way. Christianity will get in step with the times. In the word "love" sufficient arguments will be found to adapt doctrine to the new behavior. The notion of sin will be removed from sexual activities. Sexual practices will no more be judged than breathing or heartbeats. When repression disappears aberrations will decrease, and at some given moment they will lose their designation as such.

The Death of Romeo and Juliet

I have pointed out the probable positive aspects of this drastic change. But it also has one drawback; Romeo and Juliet will die once and for all. Calisto and Melibea, Tristan and Iseult, Abélard and Héloise will be buried forever. Our great lovers, our eternal sweethearts, took on gigantic proportions when facing their obstacles, and it was there in the face of adversity that they gained heroic dimensions. If Montague and Capulet hadn't been opposed to the young lovers, if Calisto had dismissed his prejudices concerning "purity of lineage," if Tristan had been able to freely love Iseult, or if Abélard hadn't had to pay for his inevitable love for young Héloise with his castration, our marvelous myths would not exist. Repression and great pain made Garcilaso passionately weave his Eclogues dedicated to Isabel Freyre. Would Dante have written the Divine Comedy if he hadn't been smitten with desire for Beatrice? Children's literature points out an obvious symptom: the story ends when happiness begins, when the royal couple gets ready to begin a happy dull married life. Man's interest goes only up to that point--until Romeo dies of love; until Calisto lies mangled at the foot of the wall. Can the reader imagine how horrible a satisfied Romeo would be? A Calisto living free in concubinage with Melibea? It can't be. There will be nothing left of that passionate rebellion now incongruous with our times. A tiny round inoffensive pill mercilessly crushed all of them.

THE REVOLUTION OF APPEARANCES

As a consequence of the new sexual morality which is more open and less demanding, the archetypes have varied. It goes even beyond that. The total concept of beauty has changed. Every era has established its own aesthetic canons. Ugly and beautiful are mere consequences of our particular appreciation at a given moment. A fat matron lifted from a Renaissance canvas would be condemned to become an old maid in today's world. Beyond any shadow of doubt, this very instant is incubating aesthetic values that will reign in future generations. Scarcely a few years ago a handsome man was considered handsome because he resembled to a certain degree the Hellenic pattern of masculine beauty: tall, muscular, young, clean, and of noble expression. Women were beautiful for more or less the same reasons. Today, the slovenliness of the hippies, their sickly faces topped off with dark glasses and matted hair are the beauty standards presently in force. In searching for new aesthetic values they have gone to the opposite extreme.

Painting, that marvelous barometer of society, passed through a stage called "op-art." In other words, optical art. Pictures appear to be something they aren't. Hallucinating plays of optical illusions deceive our poor eyes with oscillating lines and colors that appear to be painted with quicksilver. While painting is seeking out a more illustrious route, op-art points out to us with its abbreviating fantasy the lunar generation's inner soul, and, with its paucity of imagination, it indicates their temporary character of mere transition.

These youths, not content with their pale spectral faces, get together around strobe lights that make them change appearances with every flash from the bulb. The decor is so designed that nothing appears to be what it is, as if none of them accepted what they were. Drugs play a great part in sustaining the aesthetic revolution. Hallucinogens provide elephants in the air and pathways paved with blue leaves, the ultimate in visual effects. That's the shortest way to break with yesterday's cultural patterns. The deplorable use and abuse of drugs is perfectly congruent with the general picture. It rhymes with "op art" and with the defiant matted hair.

Where will we all end up? We'll have to wait about fifteen years to know the destiny of the lunar generation. In any case, culture and civilization haven't become bogged down as people are fearfully saying. Some headway has been made in new directions. Humanity has rounded a curve on a road which no one is familiar with. In the risk that this embodies is the incentive of years to come. Any attempt to stall this liberalizing route will be useless. Perhaps a review of the history of pornography will help convince us. At least it will be amusing.

COMMENTS ON THE HISTORY OF AMERICAN PORNOGRAPHY

Millimeter by millimeter skin began creeping into the movies. No matter what kind of picture it is--cowboy, Roman, karate, gangster or what have you--it runs the risk of becoming a gynecological guidebook. The bourgeois are shocked and the communists run away aghast. Bourgeois morality, capable of negotiating anything, is more flexible. The battle between the censors and the boobs will be entered in the annals of human tenacity. It lasted almost 40 years. The boobs finally won out. The first blow was almost imperceptible; it was through a filmy negligee that fluttered in the soft light. That dark protuberance was there. The spectators swallowed dryly. Then there was a fleeting glimpse in a "French" movie. It was back in the 50's when the French were still exploiting the legendary fame of Pigale and when the dry cough of Marguerite Gautier, the most famous source of infection that western culture can recall, still could be heard. The French gradually lost out to the Nordics and the Gringos. The most concrete evidence of this is the long lines of Frenchmen waiting in front of the porno movie houses in Copenhagen. If Toulouse-Lautrec were to come back to life, he would die of embarrassment. Today the Moulin Rouge is a Ursuline convent. The Byzantine struggle between censors and boobophiles gave way to an epic battle for the pilose zone located south of the waist. Abrupt and curly terrain. Dangerous ambushes. The boobophiles were made bold by the quick victory in the area of the rear guard. The censors hardly bothered to fight. They had been overcome by fatigue. They finally gave in. Spectators faced in panavision and stereophonic sound what anatomy with wild linguistic invention calls the "mons pubis." At some point in the future we will have to face such unbelievable metaphors as "Eustachian tubes" or "Fallopian tubes" or the "Turkish saddle" with the same criteria that we analyze the boldest poetry of Rimbaud or Artaud. (Who was the first sex maniac that called that puny equilateral triangle that grows under the navel "Venus's mound"?)

The funniest part of this whole comedy between bourgeois morality and its opponents lies in the ticklish distinction between art and pornography. The Supreme Court of the United States ruled after a heated discussion that pornography was that which stimulated the sexual appetite, and the rest was art. A worthless opinion. For example, when you're an adolescent a few inches of skin is all it takes to stimulate your sexual appetite while in old age you need a few square yards. In addition, there's the matter of individual preferences. How many remember that delightful Italian comedy about the guy accused of raping a hen and the explanation that he gave? "Well, your honor, the hen began moving about slowly in front of me, cackling and looking me straight in the eye, and well, after all, your honor, I'm not made of stone." Some aren't made of stone when it comes to knees, others go for thighs, and others, like our Italian, are quite content with hens.

To be honest, there is no border between pornography and art. When bourgeois society can no longer find arguments to continue censorship, it will declare that boobs or what have you have become art. That's not serious. The honest thing to do is recognize that we're dealing with an image that's sexually exciting and that a substantial part of society enjoys looking at it. The honest thing is to admit that it's a matter of pornography, eroticism or whatever you want to call it. The fact is that an enormous percentage of the population finds attractive the sight of the nude human body and couples that are sexually excited. Apparently passive contemplation increases the sexual appetite of voyeurs, which could be healthy for couples a little bored with their amatory routine. More and more frequently psychologists are recommending pornography--whether artistic or otherwise is purely subjective-- as therapy for impotence, frigidity, and plain old sexual indifference. It seems that the patients readily take to the medicine. It's better than castor oil. Then what are we to do about this "wave of eroticism that is invading us"? The same thing that you do with all waves: float on them, play with them, and don't take them too seriously. Sex has been removed from ethics, and it's not wise to go around haggling with the sun about a few inches of human skin. In a few years such attitudes will be ridiculous.

VIII

EXPEDITION IN SEARCH OF THE NEW AMERICAN MAN

SUPERWORKERS

We looked for him everywhere in the communist antipodes, and as it turns out we find the new man emerging in capitalistic society. I don't know if he's better simply because he's new--a very shaky hypothesis--but there's no doubt at all about his being different in the areas that interest socialist theoreticians: his attitude toward property, class, and nation. His attitude concerning private property will be taken up shortly. Right now let's take a look at "class" and "nation."

The big corporation has created some creatures known as executives who feel no strong need to accumulate capital. They are content to climb the managerial hierarchy by jumping from one company to another. This efficient and aseptic creature had just as soon sell soap in Detroit as cameras in Madrid. He has mastered sales, productive, marketing, and administrative techniques which work with the same degree of success in almost any corner of this planet. In the select world of these multinationals, it's not unusual today for one of these superworkers to be recruited from a company whose main office is located in Amsterdam, New York, or London. His preference is determined by salary and fringe benefits. The superworker is selling his job as a commodity to the highest bidder. He is renting his time at the highest possible price without taking into consideration the _petit bourgeois_ concern for his "fatherland." It's the case of the first workers--executives are workers too--who are truly international.

PRIVATE PROPERTY WAS THEFT

Would you believe me if I said that this particular Yankee believes less in private property than his Soviet contemporaries? Evidently not. An explanation is needed. Let's take a look.

Owning property, besides being robbery, is sheer stupidity. It's impossble to "own" things. It's possible to use them either individually or collectively, to transfer them, sell them, exchange them for other things, but "to own" a castle or an automobile is just a conceptual illusion. Legal and not human terminology. Nevertheless, until just recently man suffered from the illusion that he "owned" property simply because his goods--things, land--survived him. The human animal was so dumb that he assumed that if he owned property when he died, it was a sign of superiority. He failed to realize that the mere fact that he could take only his own bones with him to the grave proved just the opposite. The peculiar economic organization of the developed capitalistic countries, especially the United States, with long term credit plans for short lived goods is uprooting the idea of ownership and replacing it with usufruct. Americans are increasingly renting cars and houses instead of buying them. In a fluid society like this one, it was to be expected that the sharpest citizens would realize that the "ownership" of property was likely to become an unfortunate disadvantage. By owning property that ties you down to a certain place or forces you to have a particular life style you limit your future possibilities. The latter very obviously applies to the individual, but it also applies to businesses. American industry realized long ago that equipment becomes obsolete and breaks down; therefore, it's useless to try to own it. A machine that moves its pistons so many times per minute has a lifespan of x amount of time, and when that time comes, it has to be replaced. In other words instead of buying a machine you buy x number of hours of use on a certain machine. This simple observation gave rise to the practice of leasing or renting equipment. What kind of "concept" of private property can exist in an operation where salaried executives use someone else's funds (the bank's) to finance the leasing of equipment for a certain amount of time? The private ownership that Proudhon-Marx talked about was not this socialistic invention of modern capitalism but the primitive version where man was attached to his land, his castle, or even his factory.

A disquieting paradox becomes immediately apparent: the most effective enemy of private ownership is consumer society. By so much owning, discarding, and replacing in a never-ending sequence, we wind up not having the slightest attachment to material goods. A South American or even a European will talk about <u>his</u> furniture or <u>his</u> car while a <u>Gringo</u> will simply say <u>the</u> furniture or <u>the</u> car. The unnatural relationship between man and things becomes even weaker in a society when the individual doesn't consider goods that are imminently and inexorably perishable his own.

At the beginning of these thoughts I mentioned that I felt sure that private ownership meant more to a Soviet citizen than it did to an American. Now you can see why. The Soviet citizen still lives in a stage of underconsumption without access to goods that Americans squander and is subjected to a standard of living which is quite limited. A Russian, unlike a Yankee in his own country, cannot pack his bags and move at will from Kiev to Leningrad or from Moscow to the Ukrainian countryside. This (more or less respectable) immobility and poverty is what keeps alive his passion for the possession of property.

Man doesn't discard age-old customs simply because some more or less well-intentioned theoretician dictates certain ethical norms, but because society noticeably modified his habits. If Marxism hasn't triumphed in the United States today, it's not because its society is subject to the fetishes of private ownership, but because respect for individual freedom is too widespread. I don't think there's a place on this planet--excluding Scandinavia, which is a kind of United States without ghettos--where the compulsion to own (not to consume) is at a weaker point. I'm not saying that at the heart of post-industrial capitalistic society and as a result of it there is emerging a feeling of human solidarity stemming from socialism. What I am saying is that this absurd passion to own property is simply being replaced by usufruct of goods. That instrument is called money, or credit, which is the equivalent of potential money. But private ownership is steadily becoming less important. If Proudhon could see it, he wouldn't believe it.

THE EXTREMES BECOME CONFUSED

This displacement of capitalistic mentality in directions difficult to predict a few decades ago coincides with obvious movement toward typically capitalistic formulas of production in the countries of the Socialist bloc. A few years ago, almost simultaneously, the United States and the Soviet Union announced important economic measures. Nixon, who was president at that time, described a vast plan to aid the poor which would practically eradicate the nation's poverty. To the poverty stricken, up to $1,500 in economic aid would be given annually as well as food of the highest quality and preschool education so that their children would truly have equal opportunities. If the father didn't have enough vigor, cunning, knowledge, or luck to get the family on its feet and going, then the government would do it. Under the old rules of capitalism the first one read: "each one according to his own efforts." Today, there's no doubt about it, it's been hybridized with the socialist maxim "each one--at least-- according to his own needs." To be absolutely truthful, this adaptation doesn't jeopardize the capitalistic regime at all inasmuch as this system is so dynamically put together that it can be adapted to any new circumstances.

On the other hand, for the communists trapped in their Marxist dogmatism it's extremely difficult to bring about any kind of significant change. During the first part of October, 1969, the Brezhnev-Kosygin duet announced that a pilot plan with material incentives for workers had been an economic success and was being extended to all areas of Soviet production. In addition, the amount of production would be gradually determined by the relationship of supply and demand, the backbone of the capitalistic system, and not by the criteria of the "party."

In other words, after half a century of Marxism the Russians have discovered that two premises of Marx were false: proletarian man doesn't work because of some philanthrophic sense of collective responsibility but so that he and his family can live better; and that inflexibility in programming industry, far from avoiding economic chaos and improving distribution of wealth, tends to create a parasitic bureaucracy that obstructs the progress of the nation. The Russians have definitely stopped being Marxists and have abandoned the quest for a communistic society. This new policy that they have been experimenting with for years is nothing more than state capitalism. The great lord of the manor is the one who can have his workers exiled to Siberia or condemned to forced labor.

It's logical to ask on what ethical and philosophical basis Russia is relying to justify her dictatorship since she has adopted capitalism. The answer seems obvious: none. Communism, the Marxist-Leninist ideology that they will continue using, will be just a pretext for a small group-- in this case the military hierarchy--to wield power with an iron hand. The method will be Henry Ford's; the disguise, Karl Marx's.

AMERICAN TIME

First a digression on time concerning a recent piece of news. Newton vs. Einstein. An old dispute. Einstein won. A short while ago the "Theory of Relativity" was transferred from the column of hypotheses to the column of demonstrations. As we now know, time is not an imaginary dimension in which the transformation of things is parcelled out. It's not a subtle invention--like geometry or mathematics--for dismantling the mechanism of reality. We are--everything that exists--mass, time, and motion. All interwoven. Everything subject to an inexorable interaction. My five minutes used to write these notes are minutes only within a given frame of reference. My months and my years are dependent on the velocity and direction of my movement in relationship to the stars. A mirror--that spiteful indicator of grey hair, wrinkles, and other biological trickery--reflects images that are slippery and ambiguous. At a different velocity the reflection would be different. It's frightening to know for a fact that this hot Madrid of today would not be, for a hypothetical observer who is moving at a different speed, the same Madrid that I'm looking at through this window but Madrid back in 1936 or Madrid during the time of Philip II. Time is money. Another silly British saying. Time is time, which is worse.

Now that the "Theory of Relativity" has been proved, how many people will there be left in the world prone to give straightforward exact answers? How many men will feel that they are masters of absolute truths and unquestionable revelations? How many will retain as part of their vocabularies words like certainty, axiom, infallibility and other such boastful affirmations which they use as the final blow in their arguments? Will the infinitely dogmatic fauna continue to bellow without making any concessions? Will there still be serious and respectable gentlemen who pound emphatically on the table with their fists to support their infallible statements? Will they--along with Einstein--ever discover that the absolute doesn't reside within our Universe, that it simply doesn't exist?

Vain presumptuous questions! The "Theory of Relativity" will be incorporated into the textbooks of physics just as the "law of gravity" and the "Pythagorean theorem" were. Nothing will change as far as the substance of human nature is concerned. We unfeathered bipeds will go on destroying "Mistaken Enemies," vociferating "Indisputable-Truths," killing or being killed by God knows what "Indisputable Syllogisms." In the final analysis it makes no difference whatsoever that Einstein was right.

Even though we may choose to discard it, without a great deal of fuss we have come up with an extremely useful definition of time, that imaginary rhythmic dimension in which things are transformed. In fact the only thing that we perceive is the transformation of things. It seems obvious, although it may contradict Einstein, that time could not exist in an immutable universe. Enough metaphysics. Let's get back to the _Gringos_. A culture frenetically changing must change its perspective of time. I dare say that the inner time mechanism of the Yankee is different from ours. That particular world that changes, tears down, and builds anew has produced a creature that is more sensitive to time than we are. Let me see if I can explain this with a few examples. When Ortega systematized his study of history on the basis of generational groups separated by a span of fifteen years, he didn't anticipate that the acceleration of changes would shorten the time gap between generations. If up until Ortega's time generational caravans--to use one of the metaphors from his repertoire--ran in fifteen year spans, nowadays perhaps we should speak in terms of five years or less. In the Yankee's frenetic minute there is practically a generation gap between contemporaries. At times a difference of two or three years is enough to make conversation become tense. And the tendency is toward acceleration, toward change, toward a world that doesn't flow along placidly but one that's made of luminous moments of flashes. This continuous acceleration tends to reinforce itself and its consequences can be tremendous. When the Yankee specimen of the 60's and the 70's thinks about "his" time, few memories will come to mind. What time, if the vertiginous world in which fate has placed him hasn't given him sufficient quiet to incorporate a static image into his memory? What time, if adolescence--the period that we call _our_ time-- is a succession of groups that last for extremely brief periods? If up until now culture has been the result of tradition plus innovation, the formula will have to be changed. Our time--the age of the _Gringos_

--doesn't produce traditions. It's incapable of becoming bogged down in myths that are assimilated and passed on. It's an epoch in which everything is disposable. Not only the packaging, but music, books, and styles. The possibility of some form becoming classic no longer exists. Writers no longer seek immortality but momentary fame. That's all they want. One of them, Norman Mailer, has said that very soon all of us will be able to be famous for 5 minutes. What he didn't say was that soon we won't be able to be famous for much more than those five minutes mentioned in his joke. Classicism is dying. Reluctantly, the cadaver of the hallowed classics is dragged around when possible, but without the reverence that such rites require. The prelude to the definitive burial of Beethoven was his debut on a sweat shirt. It won't be long before his memory is condemned to death. Tradition is fighting with a fulminating protean society, and in the long run tradition will loose out. Tomorrow will be based on today and not some remote yesterday. It's no wonder then that concepts so closely associated with tradition such as "fatherland" and "nation" have been tremendously weakened in the United States. Things of that sort are antediluvian rhetoric.